GEORGE BUTT

MEMORIAL VOLUME

CENTENARY EDITION

Frontispiece

From A Group of Folk-Dancers

GEORGE BUTTERWORTH
MEMORIAL VOLUME

CENTENARY EDITION

YOUCAXTON PUBLICATIONS

OXFORD & SHREWSBURY

This edition transcribed, edited and arranged by Wayne Smith.

ISBN 978-1-909644-63-2
Printed and bound in Great Britain.
Published by Wayne Smith 2015
YouCaxton Publications

Contents

Photographs

Two Taken in Childhood,

One at Eton (Speech Day)

One at Leeds (1913), and

One Folk Dancing at Stratford-on-Avon

George Butterworth

1885 – 1916

"Under the wide and starry sky
Dig the grave and let me lie:
Glad did I live and gladly die,
And I laid me down with a will."

R.L.S.

INTRODUCTION

by Wayne Smith

This began in the way these things tend to, as a discovery. It was one which gradually unfolded, rose almost imperceptibly from beneath a surface, where glimpses of music - passing refrains heard on the radio - caught and held me. There was the growing sense of a particular soundscape, one that strangely I seemed to recognise and felt I already knew, though listened to for the first time. It was something I took to…inescapably. Then those songs, haunting and beautiful, words phrased and set with piano in such a way that they left me equally spellbound.

In time, and at some stage, the recognition of a name behind it all…Butterworth…George Butterworth….

Before long the interest became a passion and I found that I needed to know more about the man and the times in which he lived. What I eventually gathered, particularly from the pages of this *Memorial Volume*, made as strong an impression upon me as the music had; left me struck at the incredible life that had been lived here and the unique personality presented page after moving page in its eulogies, appreciations and the fine biographical portrait presented by R.O. Morris in the opening 'Memoir'. For George not only composed some of the most enchanting and acclaimed English music of his time, but is now recognised as an important figure in the early 20th century collecting and preserving of English folksong. He was also a founder of the English Folk Dance Society and considered one of the most accomplished Morris dancers of his generation. Furthermore, an old Etonian educated at Oxford, he had signed up with a group of pals and ended up in charge of a unit of Durham miners who fought to the bitter end at the very edge of the very worst action that took place on the battlefields of the Somme.

In short, a man of music and dance who learnt to become a soldier and a leader of men; one who, in the weeks leading up to his death, had been awarded two Military Crosses and put forward for a third. A war hero whose body was laid to rest in the field where he lay, the site marked by a simple wooden cross, never to be rediscovered or reclaimed. I was captivated, as many others have been and continue to be so to this day, though I struggle to express in words the mystery of this enduring appeal. After all I am no musicologist, simply one who has found something particularly poignant and moving about George and his music, something that speaks to me about the landscapes, the nature and the folk of England and this English countryside in which it has its roots.

As such, I like to try and imagine something of that which George must have experienced himself on those long expeditions made into the heart of Edwardian England collecting folksong and dance...wandering as he would the hamlets and greens, country lanes and ancient byways, the hidden churches and inns, the hedgerows and orchards; perhaps composing - creating as he journeyed on foot or on bike - in movement, his head full of sunlight and stars, wildflowers and whispering leaves; singing, shaping his songs, as he tramped the dales and the downs, through the hangers and hollow ways, to himself and to the trees, to the passing clouds, the wayside cherry blossom... And, maybe, to a crescent moon glimpsed low in the sky at the dimming-dusk of a man's last day, or to the first notes of a bird's song in the eggshell-blue dawn of his final hour....

The significance of the *Memorial Volume* soon became clear to me, for reference to it was made in almost everything of a biographical nature that I read about George. The reason is quite simple: within its covers are to be found a wealth of information and recollections about his life and works, to the extent that it has become the seminal source that biographers have used and refer back to in their research and writing over the years. And, at the heart of it all, George's own *'War Diary and Letters'* - a document of historic importance publicly available here in its entirety for the very first time.

The book was brought together by his father, Alexander Kaye Butterworth, who had also lost Julia, his first wife and George's mother, in 1911. Perhaps it was one way a grief-stricken parent was able to find some solace in the despairing loss of an only child. He had, no doubt, the help of the friends and family for whom it was privately published in 1918 (by *Delittle, Fenwick & Company* - publishers based in 'York and London'). The original print run was for 100, though the whereabouts of only a handful are known to exist today. In 1948, shortly after the death of R.O. Morris, who was possibly instrumental in helping put the first edition together, there was a re-print of a quantity unknown.

It was while I was carrying out research for a novel in 2011, that I discovered Cecil Sharp House (the home of the English Folk Dance and Song Society) held a rare copy of the

Memorial Volume, one I would actually be allowed to hold and read. Entering the cloistered stillness of its book-lined 'Vaughan Williams Library' has continued to be a pleasure on the occasions I have subsequently visited there, and the helpfulness of the staff has been greatly appreciated over the years.

It was a former head librarian who put me onto Hugh Butterworth. Now in his eighties, Hugh is George's cousin from his father's second marriage. I intended to use some of the material from the Memorial Volume in my novel and so sought his approval. After the exchange of a few pleasant letters, I assumed this would be the end of our contact. That was, until the August of 2014, when I decided to tour the Somme battle sites. Purely by chance we arrived in Pozieres, close to where George had been killed, just in time for its annual Butterworth memorial event. I was even more delighted to find that Hugh was guest of honour. The reconnection made, I eventually broached with him an idea I'd had of putting the Memorial Volume into the public domain. Hugh seemed interested and, following a further exchange of letters back in the UK, he suggested we discuss it more over lunch.

And so, I received the blessing which I felt necessary for this undertaking. He also agreed to my idea of moving the 'Postscript' from its original position at the end of the volume and including two new sections not found in the original: the first a record of the official 'Battalion War Dispatch' for the morning of the 5th August, 1914 (passed on to me by Hugh himself); the second a list - reflecting the headstones found in Commonwealth war cemeteries - of those friends of George's who were also levelled by war.

This anniversary edition has been produced to mark the centenary of George's death; it is also, I would like to think, a tribute to all those countless others whose place of rest, like his own, remains unknown to this very day. Those for whom George Butterworth's *Banks of Green Willow* has become an unofficial anthem.

A REMINISCENCE

by Hugh Butterworth

Two members of my family were lost during the First World War, my half-brother Hugh died near Ypres in September 1915 and my first cousin George was killed on the Somme in August 1916.

As I grew up I naturally first learned about Hugh, how he died near Hooge and that his name was on the Menin Gate. It was only later that I became aware of George, partly because his music would be played from time to time.

In the mid 1980's I discovered those travel agencies which had sprung up to deal with the increasing interest in the First World War. On one occasion I joined a group who were concentrating on the Poets of the Great War, and this was expanded to include George. I remember that we were standing near to where George had been killed...the Tour Leader started to play a recording of "The Banks of Green Willow" and a skylark rose singing into the clear blue sky.

Obviously I never knew George, but I did know his father Sir Alexander Kaye Butterworth, or to me "Uncle Alick". I first met him when my Mother and I stayed at his house in Hampstead; I was only seven and remember little of the visit. However, a few years later Uncle Alick came to visit my Father at our home in Devon. I recall that I was tremendously impressed by the small silver medallion which hung from

Uncle Alick's watch chain. It enabled him to travel free on all the railways in the United Kingdom. I was also impressed by the message on the back which offered the finder a reward of five shillings (25 pence), which at the time represented to me a serious amount of money!

I met Uncle Alick a few more times, twice he invited my brother and myself to stay with him for our half-term weekend. On one occasion he escorted me across London on my return to school; he treated me to lunch and then took me to hear Big Ben chime the hours. This was a great wartime symbol, as the chimes of Big Ben preceded the news bulletins to the people of Occupied Europe and helped to give them hope.

Uncle Alick had surprising energy for an old man and great enjoyment of life. Before the War he liked to wander round the Bank Holiday Fair on Hampstead Heath. He was also a kind and generous man and he helped a large number of people including myself. In January, 1946, I attended Uncle Alick's funeral. Two hymns were sung:- 'Abide With Me' and John Bunyan's poem, "He who would valiant be," which had been set to music by George's friend, Ralph Vaughan Williams, who was also present.

My increasing interest in George received a big boost when, in 2008, I was traced by a remarkable Frenchman M. Yves Potard. Every other year eighty of the villagers of Pozieres put on, under Yves direction, a two hour *son et lumiere*, two scenes of which are devoted to George. One showing him joining the army and the other dealing with his death in action. Yves followed the Battalion Diary of the action almost to the letter. Yves also arranges an annual ceremony which is held at the site of the memorial to George at Pozieres on the Sunday nearest to 5th August, the date of George's death. Preparations are already under way for the commemoration which will take place on the one hundredth anniversary in 2016.

The recent discovery of correspondence shows that in the months after the outbreak of war in 1914, Blake's poem 'Jerusalem' was becoming more and more popular. The Poet Laureate, Robert Bridges, wrote to Hubert Parry and asked him if he could set the poem to music. Parry replied saying that he was too busy and suggested that Bridges approach George Butterworth. Bridges wrote to Uncle Alick who replied saying that George would be unable to undertake this as he was already serving with his regiment in France, and in the end Parry did it himself. So instead of 'Jerusalem arr. Parry', it could have been 'Jerusalem arr. Butterworth'!

Even more recently, an unfinished piece of George's music which was previously unknown – 'Fantasia' for Orchestra – has been completed by the supremely talented musician and composer Kriss Russman, and it is hoped that it will be given its world premiere in the near future.

I know that Uncle Alick would have been very pleased and, also, very moved to know that so many people wished to remember his son so many years after his death.

From an Early Portrait by Miss Wigan

MEMOIR BY R.O.M.

George Butterworth was born in London on July 12th, 1885, so that he was just over 31 years of age when he fell near Pozieres on the 5th August, 1916. The greater part of his boyhood was spent at York, where his parents lived from 1891 to 1910, his father being successively Solicitor and General Manager of the North Eastern Railway. Of this period a York friend writes: "I have a clear memory of George as a little boy, independent and thoughtful beyond his age, and most interesting to watch." These early years in the North were probably not without influence on Butterworth's character, for he was temperamentally far more akin to the North than to the South, and although he often delighted to style himself a Cockney, the rugged folk of Yorkshire and Durham, with their downright manners and independence of outlook, were always peculiarly congenial to him, notably so throughout the time of his military service.

His first school was Aysgarth, the well-known preparatory school in Yorkshire. There he showed fair promise as a scholar; he was captain of the school for his last two terms and in 1899, when he entered for the Eton Foundation Scholarship, he more than fulfilled the hopes of his friends by coming out fourth in the list. One of the Aysgarth master's of that time writes of him:-

"It might well be no easy task to draw on one's memory for some account of a particular boy, whose time at his Preparatory School ended nearly twenty years ago. But I can vividly recall George. He came to school rather late accustomed to the society of older people and unversed in school fashions. But he was a clever lad and soon made his way among his fellows, and latterly took the lead and was much looked up to by the younger boys. His undoubted popularity was largely based on his kind and willing helpfulness to new comers and those who might for any reason be at a disadvantage. Admiration for his striking musical talents (on occasion he could be left in charge of the organ in chapel) and his prowess at cricket no doubt further contributed to the same end. I remember so well going with him to Eton for his scholarship examination, and can recall how his sensitive nature responded to the amount of success or failure that he assigned to himself on each paper, as we talked it over. He was so anxious to gain his object and so keen to conceal his anxiety. In short he stands out in my recollection as one of the remarkable characters in a long list and I felt sure that he would make his mark in whatever career he decided upon."

At Eton he took part with credit in the intellectual, social and athletic life of the School, and was described by the present Head Master of Eton (who became "Master of College" while Butterworth was there) as "a great fact" in College. But as a scholar he did not achieve the success his friends expected, and when he went up to Trinity College, Oxford, in 1904, he went as a commoner. The fact was, his chief interest lay elsewhere, for he was beginning to realise, probably unconsciously, that music already claimed him for her own. Without showing what could be called precocity, he had from early childhood displayed a marked aptitude for, and love of, music. He was well grounded by his mother, herself a musician of talent and distinction, and while at Aysgarth used to send home small hymn-tunes, always composed without help from the piano. In earlier days, when quite a small boy, he surprised his father by playing a childish piece, "Rousseau's Dream," in twelve keys. His father had the day before promised him five shillings as soon as he could do this and was surprised at the money being claimed so quickly. The boy, however, merely remarked that the reward seemed too much for so simple a task – exactly the comment, one feels, that he would have made twenty years later. He continued his musical studies at York under Mr. C.G. Padel, a teacher of high aims and generous ideals, to whom he owed much, and for whom he always cherished an affectionate regard. At Eton, his talent developed in various ways, and he became a prominent figure in the musical life of the School. From 1902 to 1904 he was "Keeper of the College Harmonium," and for two years was a member of the Musical Committee; on at least one occasion he appeared as a performer at one of the Eton Musical Society's Concerts. Most significant of all he began to carry a musical notebook about with him and jot down ideas as they occurred. Some of these (made during a holiday with his parents in Scotland) were later worked up into his first serious composition, a Barcarolle for Orchestra, which was played at an Eton Concert in 1903, Butterworth himself conducting. Mr. T. F. Dunhill, under whom he studied at Eton, mentions a violin sonata as having also been composed at this time. Unfortunately no trace of these pieces can now be found.

The years at Oxford (1904-1908) were essentially a logical development of his Eton career, though perhaps not especially momentous. They were above all a period of development, in which the end to be sought was not primarily knowledge, but wisdom, that is to say, an understanding of what things in life were really worthy of attainment and what were not. The usual academic studies were still followed, and followed with honesty and a fair measure of success, but neither his tutors nor anybody else imagined that his place in the class lists (second in Moderations and third in "Greats") gave any criterion of his real powers. This was fully recognised by all who knew him and was felt to be inevitable in the circumstances, a view which is borne out by a letter from his "Greats" tutor, who says:

"Like all his friends I had great admiration for George, and I greatly enjoyed, too, all the work which we did together when he was reading for 'Greats.' It of course goes without saying that his 'class' did not represent his ability, and I realised all the time that, though he took very real trouble with his Schools work, the bulk of his energy went – quite rightly – into his music."

His influence on Oxford music was remarkably strong for one who was still an undergraduate. As President of the University Musical Club his fearlessness of thought and speech made him, as might be expected, both friends and enemies, but even those whom his frankness offended could not fail to recognise his strength of mind and his singleness of purpose. The President of his College describes him as being "shy and reserved" at this time, adding that the men who knew him at all well – both dons and undergraduates – "felt real affection for him."

It was in his Oxford days that Butterworth first met Vaughan Williams and Cecil Sharp, two men whose friendship exercised a marked influence on the bent of his musical development. There was already dormant in him a strong sense of the value of nationality both in art and in life. Under the stimulus of these two friendships this sense was quickened until it became the very mainspring of his musical being. Music, revealed anew in the ancient songs and dances of the English people, showed him an ideal hitherto unguessed at, and if this ideal often tortured him by its elusiveness, to the end it remained a source of inspiration. Two Oxford friends must also be specially mentioned here in connection with his musical development. – Dr. H. P. Allen, of New College, a vivid and inspiring personality, to whom Oxford music owes more than can ever be told and to whom Butterworth constantly turned for counsel and criticism, and F. B. Ellis, of Christ Church, a devoted enthusiast, who enlisted with Butterworth soon after the outbreak of war, was with him throughout until Butterworth was killed, and was himself killed some weeks later. To both of these Butterworth was bound by the closest ties of friendship, as they were to one another; both recognised from the first the tremendous force and sincerity of his mind, the simplicity of his heart, and the originality of his creative power.

During his four years at Oxford music obtained an immensely strong hold upon Butterworth's thoughts and ambitions, and before he went down he had practically abandoned the idea, at one time entertained, of going to the bar, and had decided that music in some form or other was to be his life's work. The only question was, in what form? Music meant for him, first and last, composition; but he also felt strongly that it is a man's duty to be self-supporting, and he knew that no serious musician can hope to live by composition. Some other form of musical activity, such as criticism or teaching, seemed at first to provide a practical way out of the difficulty. With this view Butterworth, on leaving Oxford, for a short time acted as one of the musical critics for the "Times," in which capacity he showed a surprising breadth and certainty of judgement for so young a man, and a most unfaltering denunciation of anything false or meretricious. But this work soon proved uncongenial. Later, when a post as music master at Radley was offered to him, he decided to accept it, in the hope that teaching would prove less irksome than criticism.

The impression made at Radley may be gathered from the following note written by one who was a master there at the time:-

"We saw at once that one quite out of the ordinary run of men had joined us....The outstanding quality by which Butterworth will always be remembered was personality. He had extraordinary strength of character: he had opinions and the courage of them. He looked facts straight in the face and said what he thought of them. He was utterly unable and unwilling to pretend; he was intolerant of narrow-mindedness and inefficiency. He had rough corners and a rugged directness of manner coupled with gift of keen criticism. Few men can have been worse at making an acquaintance or better at making a friend. When once he decided that he liked you, all reserve vanished and there showed a man with wide interests, wide sympathy and a stout heart.

In his work he had few opportunities of knowing the boys or of being known by them. Such opportunities as he had he made for himself, and there was a generation of Radleians who grew to know him as an enthusiastic player of games, especially of racquets and fives. We felt that we could not keep him long at Radley. His real genius was for music, and he was too big a man to live happily in small surroundings. The cloistered aloofness of school life bored him and its ecclesiasticism jarred.

I last met Butterworth on the day that he enlisted and I have since met various of his Radley friends. Not one of us was surprised at his brilliant career as a soldier. It was the man through and through to do what he knew to be his duty and to do it well. That was the stuff he was made of."

Butterworth stayed at Radley for a year (1909-1910); then he returned to London and entered as a student at the Royal College of Music. It is not clear what exactly was his object in taking this step. He had been advised that he would probably find it necessary to undertake work involving more thorough technical knowledge than he possessed, both of piano and organ playing, and possibly he had an idea that he was musically too much of an amateur, and that he would acquire at the College a more precise technique in composition. He did not, however, stay long at the College, not quite a full year. During that time he studied the organ under Sir Walter Parratt and the piano under Herbert Sharpe, and also worked at harmony under Dr. Charles Wood. Sir Hubert Parry, writing with reference to his time at the College, said that he was "one of those we looked forward to doing something individual and of fine quality."

Once more he was confronted with the old problem he had already had to face, viz., in what form was he to follow music as a career? How was he to compose and at the same time earn a living? Criticism and teaching had been tried and found wanting; he felt that they could not in the long run be reconciled – at any rate in his case – with the work of composition. Had he possessed the fluency of some of his contemporaries, he would have had no time to so torment himself. But composition was always a difficult matter to him, in spite of his technical facility. Under a somewhat gruff and imperturbable exterior there lay an ironic and fastidious temperament that could only be satisfied with the best, and directed upon itself a criticism far more searching than it would ever level at another. At rare intervals an idea would come and for a month or two, perhaps, he would work away contentedly, until the piece was finished. Then a barren period would succeed, and he would again fall to wondering how he was to justify his existence. For some time he continued to find a resource in the collection and arrangements of folk-dance, sometimes alone, sometimes in the congenial society of Sharp or Vaughan Williams or other friends. But there came a time when he felt that, so far as he was concerned at least, all that could be done had been done, and then life began to assume an aspect of increasing perplexity for him. Not that he allowed himself to become bitter or morose: his sense of humour invariably came to the rescue when things threatened to become unbearable. Only those who knew him intimately could guess at the searching's of the heart, the struggles and developments and reaction, that were taking place under that outward serenity. Yet all the time there was a steady progress toward self-knowledge and self-mastery, a more and more vivid apprehension of life's finer and more impalpable meanings. It is impossible to doubt that sooner or later he would have found the solution of his problem.

As this happened he had no need to seek further. War broke out, and life, hitherto a somewhat perplexing riddle, took on a strange and captivating simplicity. Within a month of the outbreak of war he enlisted in the Duke of Cornwall's Light Infantry; from that time onward, until his death in battle, his life is best revealed in the diary which he kept and which is here printed for his friends to read. Some things, however, they will not find in it. It will not tell them of the love which officers and men alike bore him, or of the splendid self-forgetfulness and contempt of death he showed on the battlefield. He was one of those rare spirits in whom war seemed, not merely to develop a latent faculty of courage and self-reliance, but to bring to maturity all that was best and finest. When he came home on leave, even those who knew him best were astonished at his magnificent serenity. He had come at last to the full realisation of his powers and of himself.

History will see in him a man of genius cut down in the heyday of his promise, but for the friends who mourn his loss to-day the sense of bereavement is too personal for them to think of him quite in that way. His death is to them the loss that is hardest of all to bear, even in this calamitous age – the loss of a personality unique and irreplaceable.

From a Portrait Painted from Memory by Miss Wigan

DIARY AND EXTRACTS FROM LETTERS

August, 1914 – July, 1916

War between England and Germany was declared early in August. At the time I was at Stratford-on-Avon for the sessions of the English Folk Dance Society. All the regulars and reserves were immediately mobilised, and Kitchener also issued an urgent appeal for 100,000 recruits. The creation of this new force would result in vacancies for some 2,000 officers, and my first idea was to apply for one of these. The wording and the manifesto suggested that previous experience was not essential, but this turned out to be illusory. I spent two days at Oxford making enquiries, and went so far as to send in my name – through the O.T.C. – but it was obvious that I had no chance, and I shortly heard from the Oxford authorities that they were unable to recommend me. After this I returned to Stratford, and remained there for the rest of the session. Just before leaving I got a letter from R.O. Morris, saying that he and his friend Woodhead were probably going to enlist as privates in "Kitchener's Army," and inviting me to join them. I had already made up my mind that this was the most practical and obvious way of serving the country, and I wired to Morris saying that I would like to meet him in London and discuss the proposal.

<u>1914</u>

Saturday, August 29ᵗʰ.
Returned to London and dined with Morris and Woodhead – found they had already made preliminary arrangements. They have been advised by Scotland Yard authorities to join the Duke of Cornwall's Light Infantry, as it had been decided to recruit for that regiment in large numbers, and this would give a better chance for parties of friends to join en bloc. They had already persuaded two others to come in – Keeling, a journalist, and P.A. Brown, late of New College. I said I should probably come too, but would not decide definitely until I had seen my father, who was away for the week-end.

After dinner visited Vaughan Williams, who was in great form. He had taken his family for a holiday to Margate, where he was arrested by a boy-scout while writing a lecture on Purcell; he then returned to London and became a sergeant in the Special Constabulary.

Sunday, August 30ᵗʰ.
Called on Colonel Barrington-Kennett, who was delighted when I told him I was going to enlist; he said Victor was at Dover with the Flying Corps Reserve, patrolling the Channel; Basil on the staff of the Flying Corps abroad; Aubrey at the front, with a commission.

Monday, August 31ˢᵗ.
Saw my father and fixed things up. At 12.30 went to Scotland Yard recruiting office with Brown, but we were advised to

come again early next morning to go through the medical and other preliminaries – the idea being that we should all swear in on Wednesday in a body, and be ready to start then at once. Meanwhile there have been two additions to our party, F.B. Ellis and his brother Roland, the latter having come over from British Columbia specially to fight.

Tuesday, September 1st.
Brown the two Elises and myself went early to Scotland Yard and got through the medical without difficulty. The filling in of papers took a considerable time, as there was a great crowd of applicants.

I ought to mention that just at this time there was a huge rush of recruits – on Tuesday over 4,000 joined in London alone, and in the next few days those that came in were probably as many as all those who joined during August. This was partly due to increased activity among recruiters, partly to the seriousness of the news from France, which during the week-end looked very bad.

We were not allowed to leave the office before we had actually sworn in and received our first day's pay, which we were rather unwilling to do for fear of being separated from the rest of our party; we were assured, however, that there would be no risk of this, as we were all bound for the same depot (Bodmin, Cornwall), and that it would not matter in the least if we travelled down in separate batches.

We were then given leave until 9 o'clock the next morning, and separated to make our final arrangements.

*Wednesday, September 2nd. Reassemble at **Horse Guards Parade** then* 9am. The four of us, as instructed, met at the Horse Guards Parade where there were many hundreds of recruits assembled; after considerable delay – the Bodmin men were sorted out, and marched off triumphantly to Charing Cross Underground station, headed by a brass band and much stimulated by the cheers of the crowd.

On arriving at Paddington we were allowed to scatter for lunch, and rallied again for the train to Bodmin at 1.30. We decided unanimously that the transport arrangements were not creditable to the Committee of Railway Managers. The train was an ordinary one, and the amount of space reserved quite insufficient, many having standing room only. Notwithstanding, the journey down was a hilarious one – beer and singing ad lib – it was many days before we were cheerful again. We had two changes, and did not reach Bodmin till after dark. There we were met by a sergeant and marched up without delay to the Barracks. Our reception there was not encouraging; at the gate we were each presented with one blanket, and told that the sleeping accommodation was already over-full, and that we must do as best we could in the open. Some 20 of us accordingly stationed ourselves under a small group of trees. Food was the next question; although we had been given no opportunity for a meal since Paddington, nothing was provided for us. Luckily, the canteen was still open, and by dint of much pushing we managed to secure a tin of corned beef and bottled beer. Considering the situation in which we found ourselves – the night was a distinctly cold one for September – it was not surprising that certain of the rougher specimens partook rather freely. Anyhow the result was the most extraordinary night I ever remember. Few made any attempt to sleep, and those who tried were not given much chance. It so happened that we shared our "pitch" with a rabble from Handsworth, Birmingham – a district which is, I believe, notorious. These worthies kept us supplied with a constant stream of lewdness, mostly of a very monotonous kind; there was one real humorist who made some excellent jokes, but they are scarcely repeatable. At about 2 a.m. we were joined by several unfortunates who had found their tents already occupied (by lice), and preferred the open air and the wet grass. Altogether, it was a remarkable experience, the most surprising thing about it being the complete absence of any attempt at discipline.

Thursday, September 3rd.
Morning found most of the crowd considerably sobered – not to say depressed. Breakfast was long delayed, and when it came consisted of loaves of bread thrown about indiscriminately, and large dishes of tea (mixed with milk and sugar) one dish to eight men. We eked out this allowance with the remains of last night's supper.

The proceedings of the day were irritating and futile in the extreme – endless "parades," and very little business done. Amongst other things we were all medically inspected again; this time to see if we were fit for foreign service. But, curiously enough, this inspection was much less thorough than the one in London.

Meals were a great difficulty and the conditions generally pretty bad, and I believe not a few actually deserted on their second day of service. The hopeless lack of discipline is not difficult to explain:-

The maximum accommodation in the barracks is for 500, and we were about 1,500.

1. There were only four or five N.C.O.'s to manage the lot.
2. Fresh batches of recruits were arriving daily, and corresponding detachments were being drafted to training camps.
3. The only pleasant thing about the barracks was the good temper of the N.C.O.'s, who, though hopelessly overworked, yet managed to be patient with all – or most.

The conditions, however, can only be described as disgraceful; after all, if the Government say they require half a million men they must be prepared to receive them in large numbers. If they have no room they ought to start a waiting list. I understand that Bodmin was not by any means the worst of the depots; at Reading, for instance, men had to sleep in the open without even a blanket. The conditions were all the worse because recruits had been specially told to bring next to no luggage, as they would receive their full kit directly on reaching the depot, whereas, in fact, many received nothing for days, and even weeks, and thus had absolutely no change of clothing.

In the evening general leave to go out was granted, and there was a lively time in the town. Our party took the opportunity to have a good wash and supper in the best hotel – much to the amusement of an officer who was dining at the next table. Our relations with officers are evidentially going to be amusing; in normal circumstances I should be against using our comparative wealth for acquiring luxuries which are denied our comrades, but considering the shortage of supplies of all kinds, there is no alternative.

I ought to mention that during the day we were joined by the rest of our company – augmented by an eleventh hour recruit, i.e., E.G. Toye – so that our party now was

P.A. Brown, University Teacher

G. Butterworth

F.B. Ellis, Musician

R.A. Ellis, Engineer and Farmer

F.H. Keeling, Journalist

R.O. Morris, Musician

E.G. Toye, Musician

R.C. Woodhead, Civil Servant

For the night we were put into a tent – immune from vermin of the grosser kinds – and were comparatively comfortable.

Next day, *Friday, September 4th,* we found ourselves selected to go with the next detachment to Aldershot, where we were to have our training. About 500 of us travelled by special train, this time with plenty of room. We were not sorry to leave Bodmin.

From Aldershot we marched two miles to Watts Common, and were rather pleased to find we were to be under canvas. On arriving at the camp we were served with tea and decent rations, and put into a tent with two young fellows whom we picked up on the journey – decent boys of the clerk class – by name Watts and Coat; they were subsequently "recognized" as belonging to the party.

We turned in feeling quite happy, convinced that anyhow the most uncomfortable camp in the world would be preferable to dirty and overcrowded barracks.

First days in Camp, September 5th – 17th.

As I am several days behind with this journal, it is impossible to give details of each day. I am now writing on Sunday 13th, and will try and give some sort of a summary of the intervening time.

REGIMENTAL.

At present there are seven battalions of the D.C.L.I., some of them at the front, the 6th and 7th (at least) consist entirely of recruits (with a few old soldiers), and are stationed here. We belong to the 6th, which is supposed to be the likeliest of the two!

I think there are about 1,200 in each battalion – about 200 over strength. Each battalion contains four companies; each company four platoons; each platoon four sections.

Each Company has a Captain (why we are also favoured with a Major I don't know), four lieutenants (young officers), one to each platoon, and similarly four sergeants (N.C.O.'s), who are, so to speak, parallel with the lieutenants, though under them: the function of the lieutenants seems to be to keep in touch with the captain, while the sergeants are more directly concerned with the men. That, at least, is how it strikes me at present, though I believe in the field the lieutenant directs the platoon, and the sergeant only steps in if the officer should be incapacitated.

After an incredible amount of sorting out which took, literally, days – we were at least put into platoon number 16, (i.e., the 4th of D Company, and we formed about half the last section of our platoon, i.e., the 4th section of the 4th platoon of the 4th Company), but actually they reckon everything from the company, so that our proper title is, 16th section, 16th platoon, D Company.

OFFICERS.

In addition to the above, there are several Company N.C.O's (irrespective of platoons), and several Battalion N.C.O.'s and officers (irrespective of Companies).

The man we have most to do with is our platoon sergeant, Edmunds, an excellent fellow, and very patient with his men.

We are very lucky to be under him, but as a matter of fact most of the sergeants seem to be nice men, and are doubtless chosen largely on that account.

Our platoon lieutenant, Hammond by name, is the only young officer in camp who has had any experience worth speaking of, and there again we are lucky. He also seems to be a good fellow, but of course we are not personally acquainted with him, for it is contrary to military etiquette for an officer to have any except purely official relations with privates; with Sergeant Edmunds we are respectfully familiar!

When we first came here there was a great shortage both of officers and N.C.O.'s – the vacancies have been gradually filled. Woodhead and Keeling, having had a little previous training, are now lance-corporals, and the former is our section leader. Major Barnet invited applications for commissions from the members of our party, and Toye put in for one and was promptly accepted. He is now in command of a platoon of B Company. The rest of us, after much consultation, decided that the most important thing for us was to keep our party intact; having arranged to serve together, it would obviously be unfair on those who might be left if some of us became officers – (Toye, having joined at the eleventh hour, was held to be free) – so we told the Major that unless all could have commissions, we would continue as we were; naturally enough, that was considered as equivalent to a refusal.

In the meanwhile there has been a great influx of young lieutenants, most of whom have obviously had little, if any, training; there is one who is drilling in the ranks with us, and who had to be shown how to "form fours."

How all this will turn out, heaven only knows; personally I

should feel uncomfortable at taking on a responsible job without any proper opportunity of training for it. Toye will be all right, for he is amazingly quick and facile, and full of self-confidence; but I am doubtful about some of the others.

Time Table.
This is nominally as follows :-

6am. Reveille, dress, clean up tent (a mug of tea is sometimes obtainable).
7am. Parade – usually a short march along the road.
8am. Breakfast.
9am. Parade – various kinds of drill till 1 o'clock. Half-an-hour is always given to Swedish exercises.
1pm. Dinner
2pm. Drill till 5pm.
5pm. Tea. After tea we are liable to be called upon for occasional extra work any time up to 7pm, but usually nothing particular happens.
7pm – 9.30pm. We are free to go anywhere, and usually go into the town for shopping and supper.

N.B. – The drill is never very continuous – there are occasional intervals for rest, and the easy things are sandwiched in with the more arduous movements. So far I have not once felt really tired, but no doubt they will increase the work by degrees. One thing which has kept us back badly has been the absence of boots and other equipment. The intention of the authorities is to take us on as fast as possible; comparatively little time will be given to close-order drill, which is almost useless in action.

We have already touched on things which the ordinary recruit would not begin until he had done elementary drill for many months. At the same time a certain amount of "smartness" is doubtless necessary, as it is the best and shortest way of getting men to respond to the word of command.

TENTS.

Owing to the general over-crowding we are sleeping 14 in a tent. We have been fairly lucky in our bed-fellows – for it was not possible to choose the extra ones; there are two splendid Birmingham chaps, young married working men, and two or three less desirable Londoners, of the shopkeeper class.

Personally I find lack of room almost the most uncomfortable thing about camp; owing to shortage of kit our outfit is of a very scratch order, and hard to keep tidy, in spite of a knapsack. At night we cover almost all the available floor-space, and the atmosphere is usually foggy, for it is now too cold to keep the tent open; however, we manage to keep very warm, with the help of extra rugs. All the same I frankly don't understand how so many men are expected to live in one tent. The bulk of their bodies take up most of the room, and in addition we must have – 14 rifles, 14 bayonets, 14 sets of clothing, etc., 14 blankets, 14 rugs, 14 plates, cups, knives, forks, etc., besides various odds and ends for general use.

In fine weather we manage fairly well, as we can expand into the open, but the less said about wet days the better. The effect of 14 wet people huddled together is bad for the temper.

Fortunately, when our organization was at its worst, the weather was lovely, but now the equinoctial gales have set in.

FOOD.

The three daily meals supplied by the authorities are reasonably good – one expected rough fare:-

Breakfast-Tea (so-called), bread and some tinned food.
Dinner-Stewed beef (invariable) and potatoes (ditto); for some technical reason the cooks are unable to attempt roasting.
Tea-Bread, butter (sometimes), and jam or tinned fruit. Except that there is never enough tea, these meals are fairly satisfactory. (N.B. – Nothing is supplied after 5pm.)

CANTEEN

We are supposed to be able to fill up deficiencies at the regimental canteens, of which there are three, one for beer only, and two for food, tobacco, etc. All of these are very unsatisfactory, being quite insufficiently equipped. The beer is simply not worth fighting for; and there is no other way of getting it. The "dry" canteens are always running short of everything, and there is no way of getting the cup of hot coffee or cocoa which would be so acceptable at night. For our part, we have formed a habit of going into Farnborough every evening and getting a proper supper, but there are not many who can afford that regularly.

CLOTHING.

This is the chief grievance: every recruit on enlisting was told that he would be provided with full kit immediately, and was consequently advised to bring next to nothing with him.

As a fact, for many days nothing at all was supplied; underclothing and boots are now being gradually doled out, but no khaki or overcoats; hence the men have no protection from wet and no proper change of clothes, and every shower of rain means so many more on the sick list. Here again, those with spare cash have been able to supply deficiencies, but the majority are in a poor way.

PROVISION FOR SICKNESS.

This is practically non-existent. I believe a few serious cases have been removed to hospital, but those with ordinary complaints (chills, diarrhea, etc.) can do nothing but make themselves as comfortable as possible in their own tents – no effort seems to be made to provide them with special food. There are doctors, of course, but they can do little without proper help and accommodation.

HOSPITAL ARRANGEMENTS

can only be written down as bad. There should, of course, be a hospital tent for the sick.

Watts Common, Aldershot,

17ᵗʰ September, 1914.
"This address is all right now as the postal arrangements have improved. Wet weather does not better the conditions, and a good many are down with sickness. Our tent is intact so far, thanks to superior clothing. The authorities are gradually doling out underclothing and boots, but no khaki or overcoats yet. I had to buy a mackintosh.

Am very fit – but of course there are risks, far more than in peace time. We are going to be inoculated against enteric to-day.

We are probably moving into barracks or huts very soon."

I will now return to the system of daily record.

Friday, September 18th.

Our party had its first casualty, Roland Ellis being down with a chill, or influenza. After he had spent an uncomfortable day in the tent, his brother lodged a respectful but firm protest, and got permission to remove him to a private room at Aldershot.

This, of course, was a special favour; an ordinary private would have been kept in the camp until dangerously ill.

The morning was almost entirely given up to the distribution of pay, though the weather was fine. It took nearly two hours for our company alone to get their week's money – a good instance of army red tape; it had to be done in the recognized way, any departure from which it is impossible without an order from headquarters.

In the afternoon we had our turn in the local swimming bath – an unsavory business – and later on were inoculated for enteric. This operation is similar to vaccination, and affects different men in different degrees. Irritation of the arm and occasional sickness may be expected for about two days.

The inoculation was not compulsory, but we were warned that those refusing would almost certainly be sent down to the 7th Battalion, which consists chiefly of undesirables, and will probably never be of very much use.

Our battalion is expected to be ready for foreign service soon after Christmas; personally I doubt this very much; we seem to be making very little progress, and the officers are mostly without experience.

Saturday, September 19th.

All more or less feeling effects of inoculation; an idle and uncomfortable day. No parades, but temper not improved by having to clear out the tent as usual at 6am in bitterly cold wind. Everyone very depressed and somnolent.

Sunday, September 20th.

Another idle day – the fourth in succession. Owing to absence of uniform, we are not allowed to attend church, but are given no alternative employment. The leisure would be pleasant enough, if there were any comfortable place to sit in, but the wind finds out every corner of the tent, and it is not possible to sit there except wrapped in blankets. There is a large Y.M.C.A. tent, with writing tables, but that is almost as uncomfortable, and very crowded.

In the afternoon Roland Ellis returned to the tent, having recovered very quickly from his bout of influenza, but almost at the same time Morris was knocked over with it, and was removed to a hotel at Aldershot.

The right to shift into private quarters during illness has apparently been established for our party, which is a relief, but it does no credit to the authorities.

Monday, September 21st.

The chief event was the departure of the 7th Battalion, who were moved into a new camp at Woking; their tents are to be occupied by a detachment of the Durham's, so that we shall not get any more room – in fact, at present, we are worse off, as they have taken all our blankets with them. Horse rugs have been served out instead; they are warm, but hard to keep clean.

Khaki jackets and trousers were given to most of us in in the course of the day, but no caps or puttees. In a few weeks' time we may begin to look like soldiers.

Tuesday, September 22<u>nd</u>.

A fine, sunny, windless day – immense relief – camp seems quite pleasant.

Got through some good work in the morning. In the afternoon the battalion, accompanied by a bugle band, went for its first "route march"; about eight miles along roads. Being one of the few still unprovided with boots, I was obliged to abstain, and did orderly for one day. His duties are (1) To secure the rations; (2) To wash up; (3) To keep the tent in order (more or less). In return for this work, which in present conditions is lengthy, he is excused from all drills.

Wednesday, September 23<u>rd</u>.

Sharp frost in early morning, followed by a fine, warm day. We are getting on faster with our work now, even if we don't know any of it thoroughly. In the afternoon the company carried out a sham attack. We advanced in a series of extended lines, alternating rushing forward about 50 yards, and then lying down and firing as fast as possible. Rapid fire is supposed to be the chief asset of English infantry. We have also been practicing several movements which are quite new, the result of experience of the present War. These are chiefly defensive measure against sudden attacks by cavalry or artillery.

Thursday, September 24<u>th</u>.

The question of commissions has again cropped up; we have all been wavering in our minds about it for some time, and seeing crowds of beardless youths shipped down here as officers has made us rather less satisfied with our position as privates: the climax came when the most incompetent of the lot –

who actually had his first lesson in soldiering only a few days ago in the ranks of our platoon – was officially appointed as our platoon officer, in place of Hammond, who is probably going to the front. Within the last few days several of us have been approached from different quarters on the subject of commissions. Only yesterday I had a letter from General Ovens, of the North Command, practically offering me a commission in his Brigade, the 68th, stationed at Pirbright, near here; and also asking me to name others of our party.

After some discussion, it was decided that I should follow this up, and propose the names of Morris, Brown, Woodhead and the two Ellises; as we considered it improbable that all would be accepted, I grouped the names in pairs – Morris with myself, Brown and Woodhead together, with the two Ellises together – so that no one should be left alone in the lurch.

The only remaining member of our party (Keeling) is now a corporal, and prefers in any case to remain in the D.C.L.I.

N.B. – There are no commissions vacant in our battalion.

General Ovens had told me to write to the Brigade Major at Pirbright, but, after consulting the officers here, we decided that a personal interview would be simpler. Accordingly F.B. Ellis and myself were given leave to go over to Pirbright in Eliis's motor car, which he has been keeping with permission at Farnborough. We had a memorable afternoon. At Pirbright village we stopped for a beer, chiefly for the sake of seeing once again the inside of a country inn, and arrived at the camp of the 68th Brigade at about 4.30. It is a much larger camp than ours, as it houses (!) the whole brigade – 4 battalions; on the other hand, things are obviously less advanced, not a single uniform to be seen. The Brigade Major is the Officer temporarily in charge of the whole camp, and we went off to his tent rather uncertain how to approach so exalted a person. We had no need to be nervous; the sentry, whom we had first to satisfy, turned out to be a seedy Tynesider, with a two-day's beard; an intensely comic picture. The Brigade Major himself – though more respectable – was scarcely more formidable; what is familiarly called a "dug-out";...........Like everyone else in the camp he was dressed in mufti, and appeared to be very vague on the subject of commissions. One theory of his was that all the second lieutenancies were filled up, by that we could probably become first lieutenants or even captains if we chose! Our interview was very amusing, but would not have satisfied a stickler for military etiquette. We came away with an increased respect for the organization of the D.C.L.I., and without arriving at any result, for the Brigade Major had no power to nominate us himself, and had received no instructions from General Ovens. He promised to let us know something more definite in a day or two.

Friday, September 25<u>th</u>.

We had our first firing practice, miniature range, 10 rounds each. Our lieutenant performed a remarkable feat, missing the target five times running.

Every Friday evening the cooks of D Company are in the habit of sending the hat down the lines, the implication being that the quality of next week's rations will vary in proportion to the amount collected. On this occasion a strong-minded corporal set up an objection; there was a row, the Major was summoned, and grossly insulted by the cooks, who were eventually marched off in a body to the guard room. The incident is a good illustration of the kind of petty bribery which appears to be rampant in the Army; I doubt whether even the sergeants are always above suspicion – at any rate they keep their eyes discreetly shut – and, as for these cooks, they are simply vagabond old soldiers who have re-enlisted on the chance of making a bit. "Old soldiers" have a very bad name in the present army (the term does not, of course, include those who obtained rank of any kind in their former service). Another job they take on is that of policing the camp, though why they should be chosen for this purpose is more than I can imagine. Anyhow they perform their duties exceedingly ill, and are, if anything, more easily corruptible than the cooks; a drop of whisky will help them to connive at any offense. Their nocturnal perambulations were cynically described to us by one of their number in these words: "We 'unts the bushes round the camp, and follers the sound of our own footsteps."

Saturday, September 26th.
The King visited Aldershot. In the morning the whole of our Division (16 battalions) turned out on the Queen's Parade Ground, and were inspected; i.e., the King and Staff walked once across the lines, and we presented arms – a futile proceeding, even from the point of view of the ceremonial. Considering the labour involved in getting together 16,000 men, it would surely be possible to do something more with them. Bands are apparently not used at all in war time.

Sunday, September 27th.
A lovely day, and pleasant rest. The morning casualty list contains the name of Aubrey Barrington-Kennett – the youngest and most loved of the family.

Monday 28th September.

Another fine day: in the afternoon inoculations, the second dose. Afterwards I went over to Farnborough to see Victor bk, who is now at the Headquarters of the Flying Corps. We dined with his sister-in-law.

We have now been rather more than three weeks in camp, and things are settling down; a great deal of what was at first uncomfortable has now become merely routine: at the same time we owe a lot to the weather, which except for about three days has been splendid. I still think that a spell of wet would knock most of us up: there is some talk of moving into barracks quite soon, but when is uncertain.

One curious effect on the mind of our present life is that it is almost impossible to take any interest in anything outside the camp; the War is merely a distant rumour, and intellectual activity is limited to an occasional game of chess. The continued demand for more recruits causes us all great amusement: in fact, if it were not for the discomfort, and the appearance of names that we know in the casualty lists, Kitchener's Army would seem a colossal joke.

One cannot help being struck by the absence of anything which one would ordinarily call efficiency; this may possibly be more apparent than real, and of course there may be tremendous pressure at headquarters, but all the same there is no doubt that army people dislike doing anything in a hurry; the accusation of red tape is to a great extent justified, e.g., the time wasted in sorting letters, distributing pay, etc. Economy of time does not seem to be understood at all.

A good example of red tape is the way of dealing with the casual sick list: the official army method of taking a roll of any sort is to form up in lines, and so every morning at 8.30 we hear the ludicrous order, "Fall in, the sick." I shudder to think what a civilian doctor would say if he came here on a rainy day and saw men with chills lining up in the wet, waiting to be marched off in order to the medical tent.

******

Sunday, November 15th, 1914. Bullswater Camp, Woking.

I have been asked to continue this journal, and will try to bring it up to date, though there is not much to tell.

First of all I must explain shortly how I came to be here. I think I have already mentioned that, during the first week of October, General Owens, head of the 68th Brigade, offered commissions to self and five friends. This offer was generally accepted, subject to the sanction of the D.C.L.I. officials. The latter, however, did not show us as much goodwill as I expected. Our company commander lodged an objection — trivial as well as inaccurate — on the ground that we had already been offered commissions in the D.C.L.I. and refused them. To this we replied that we had not previously been given the opportunity en bloc, and had not cared to risk breaking up the party by accepting offers singly.

The situation was a curious one. General Ovens, having once made up his mind, stood by us splendidly. I kept up communications with him by means of Ellis's motor car, which carried messages to and from Bullswater (General Ovens' headquarters) almost daily, and for a whole week a ridiculous three-cornered correspondence went on. General Ovens would send me what practically amounted to a command to join; this I passed on to the Commanding Officer, who invariably ignored it. Why he was so anxious to keep us I cannot conceive, but I fancy it was just a bluff, his only object being to save the face of our company commander by making things as difficult for us as possible.

However, to cut a long story short, one day a more than usually firm message came from the General, we were all called off parade and ordered to report ourselves as soon as possible at our new headquarters. An hour or two later the motor car, supplemented by a taxi, was conveying us and all our belongings to Bullswater Camp.

On the whole we were not sorry to leave the D.C.L.I. – I have explained why.

Of our original party of eight, two remained behind – Toye, who had been given a commission, and Keeling, who had been promoted to sergeant, and preferred to stay on.

On arriving at Bullswater, we found that matters were far from being settled. The General received us most cordially but explained, with some embarrassment, that he really did not know what to do with us now that he had got us. Owing to the delay, some of the vacancies had been filled up, and the War Office, in fact, pretended that there were none left. This he knew to be an exaggeration, but at the same time he hesitated to take us on then and there without some kind of confirmation from headquarters. In any case it was necessary for us all to go up to London to get uniform and kit, and so it was decided that we were to remain at home until sent for. To anyone who knows how the War Office usually deals with these matters, it will not seem surprising that we were kept waiting a good many days. I found the delay most demoralizing as well as annoying. After five strenuous weeks, the feeling of being absolutely idle, while

everyone else was busy, was trying in the extreme. One almost
began to share the ordinary civilian anxieties from which soldiers
in camp are quite free. Perhaps it was as well for one's intelligence
that one's interest in the war and things in general should be
revived, and I found this interest remained with me afterwards,
which shows the difference between an Officer's life and the
almost physical life of the private – at any rate under General
Watt's conditions. While in town I read Bernhardi's "Germany
and the Next War", and came to the conclusion that Germany's
crime is primarily an intellectual one – too much theory – the
doctrine of the end justifying the means is wrong, because it is
impossible to prophesy accurately what either will be.

Another rather depressing feature of London at this time was
the darkness of the streets at night – the result, apparently, of an
Admiralty order. The idea was to obliterate important landmarks
in the event of a Zeppelin raid, but is difficult to see how this
would work, and it certainly did not make things any more cheerful.

Getting uniform, etc., was not difficult; Moss Brothers,
Bedford Street, W.C. are wonderful people, and 'their Mr. Peter'
is especially wonderful – he threw things incontinently on my
back, and they just stuck there, and fitted beautifully.

I need not go into details about the tedious settlements of
our affairs….Our dispositions are as follows:-

F B Ellis, R A Ellis) 1st Lieutenants,
                              10th Northumberland Fusiliers
Woodhead) 1st Lieutenant,
                              12th Durham Light Infantry
Brown, Morris, Self) 2nd Lieutenants,
                              13th Durham Light Infantry

Originally we were all appointed 1st Lieutenants, but, as the 13th Durham's seemed to be particularly strong in junior officers, Brown, Morris and self requested to be made seconds.

Of the next four weeks I will only give a short summary. On the whole I have enjoyed it very much, chiefly because of the men whom I have had to deal – in particular, those whom I have been actually commanding. The enormous difference in the rank and file between this and the DCLI is easily explained:-

1. These men are almost all strictly local, instead of a mix-up of Birmingham, London, etc.
2. They are almost all working men (in my platoon 90% are miners).
3. They are Northerners.

Coming here was exhilarating in much the same way as detraining at Newcastle Station – everyone seemed so very much alive.

There is no doubt as raw material our men are wonderfully good – physically strong, mentally alert, and tremendously keen: they do not altogether understand the necessity for strict military discipline, but are very eager to learn their job as quickly as possible. They are also very good fellows indeed, and in short it is a great pleasure to be with them.

As to the Officers, it is difficult to form any estimate; except for the Colonel, very few have been in the regular army; a few have seen active service in South Africa or elsewhere, but the large majority have had merely Territorial or OTC experience. This is all that could be expected in the case of the subalterns, and in the 13th we seem to have a very good lot, but the lack of real military experience among the senior officers is a real draw-back.

In the present state of our training a still greater source of trouble is the inexperience of the NCO's, and here we are distinctly worse off than in the Cornwall's; many of them are merely recruits promoted, and practically none have any of the regular's snap and assurance. Perhaps the greatest surprise I had on arriving was to find that after five weeks training I knew quite as much as my company sergeants, at first this was rather a relief, but now one is beginning to wish for more support; the sergeants and corporals are mostly splendid fellows, but have very little authority.

CAMP.

Bullswater Camp contains, of course, the whole of our Brigade, the lines of the four battalions being separated from each other by a small open space. This makes about 350 living tents in all, so that we cover a considerable acreage. The men sleep 10 to 15 in a tent, and I suppose are quite as uncomfortable as we were on Watts Common. On the other hand, the marquee accommodation is very good, there being several large recreation tents, besides canteens.

The Officers sleep two in a tent, at a short distance from their respective battalions.

The worst thing about the camp is its extreme dirtiness, the natural surface being completely worn away. In September I believe the dust was fearful, and now of course, it is mud.

WORK.

On arriving I was appointed to command the 11th platoon, C Company; Morris has the 10th of the same. Our company commander is Captain Walker; second in command, Lieut. Blake, and the other two subalterns are 2nd Lieutenants Clarke and Pullen. I believe we are about the only company in the brigade with a full complement of Officers, and I am glad to say that we all get on very well together.

I ought to mention that the Commanding Officer of the 13th is Colonel Ashby, a distinguished soldier who fought at Tel-el-Kebir. We are very lucky to have such a good man, as it is probably only his age which prevented his being snapped up before.

Our second in command is Major Biddulph, also a retired regular.

The daily routine is very much the same as in the Cornwalls, about six hours' work, with occasional lectures in the evening. We are progressing, however very slowly indeed, being very badly off for equipment of all kinds. Our rifles are of an obsolete pattern, and quite useless except for drill purposes. Another serious drawback is the lack of space; there is practically no flat ground for drilling, and very little open country either.

If only we could get going, I am sure we should become efficient very quickly, as the men are very keen and physically quite first-rate.

Sunday, November 29th.

The last fortnight has been extremely trying for all of us, owing to the complete break-up of the weather; one realises now how extremely lucky we have been in this respect. The autumn being exceptionally fine, we have begun to think that after all a winter camp would be quite tolerable, but we do not think so now. Our first catastrophe occurred one very squally evening, when a sudden gust of wind carried away four of the largest marquees, burying several men beneath them. The alarm was sounded, and we swarmed on to the parade ground, but fortunately no one was hurt.

Soon after this we had a week's cold snap – unusually severe for the time of year, 20 degrees of frost being reported one night. Luckily we escaped snow, but of course hard frost under canvas is no joke, particularly because of there being no warm place to sit in.

All this time we were expecting almost daily to be called away to our winter quarters at Aldershot. Our move to Malplaquet Barracks was definitely fixed for November 16th, and the advance party had actually left, when suddenly we heard that the whole thing was postponed. Apparently the authorities were expecting a raid on the coast, and in order to facilitate the emergency transport arrangements, all other movements of troops were temporarily cancelled. It was even suggested that we might have to keep the camp going over Christmas, but fortunately this turned out to be an exaggeration.

After several false alarms our long-overdue exodus took place on the very last day of November. This was probably just in time to prevent disaster; the last few days were desperate; after the frost broke we had a bad spell of wet, which not only swamped the camp, but penetrated everything inside the tents. For several nights there was hardly a dry blanket to be had, and it is clearly impossible to carry on with that sort of thing indefinitely.

It would be difficult to over-praise the men's behaviour through all of this discomfort; I often used to go down the lines to enquire how they were getting on, and always got a cheerful answer. It is all very well to say that it is much worse in the trenches, but the men in the trenches get relieved, and there is no billeting at Bullswater. I certainly think the authorities ought to have provided extra blankets and better accommodation, and probably this would have been done, had we not been expecting to leave any day.

It is to be hoped that those who grumble at national slackness will make an exception in favour of the working people of Durham County; the large majority of these men have given up good jobs and comfortable homes for the best reasons, and are willing to stand almost anything, if only they are to be allowed to get out and finish off the war.

One other event of the last fortnight must be mentioned, namely, the retirement of General Ovens, who was reported unfit for service abroad. I think everyone was sorry to lose him, and, not least, his friends from the Cornwalls.

Monday, November 30th. The move to Aldershot.

This was rather an interesting performance, as the whole brigade marched in as a body, 100 yards separating each battalion. Appropriately enough the weather was at its worst – a gale of wind and driving rain. This did not make the job of packing and loading any easier, but by mid-day we were all ready to move off. One got some idea from this of the vast scale on which army transportation has to be worked; a brigade is, of course, a comparatively small body, and we were certainly not over-stocked in any way, but it took something like 100 traction engines and motor lorries to move our stuff. These were ranged along the road in an apparently endless line, and made us feel very important. Owing to the wet we were, of course, unable to strike camp, and a party was left behind to do this as soon as the weather allowed.

After an early dinner had been served, we marched off triumphantly in drenching rain, and so, farewell to Bullswater, and at the other end comfortable barrack rooms, and fires in each!

****

1915

Ashford, March 5ᵗʰ, 1915.

"We are here for an indefinite time – billets very comfortable, other prospects poor. No progress whatsoever to report, except that we are now khaki clad.

These strikes are a nuisance, and I see there is a small one on the N.E.R. Personally I should do three things –

1. Hang (or bayonet) all employers whose profits show an increase on previous year.
2. Imprison for duration of war all who organize cessation of labour in important industries.
3. Make Lord Robert Cecil dictator for duration of war, as being the only man in Parliament who has anything useful to say."

Ashford, 20ᵗʰ May, 1915.

"We move on Sunday to huts near Liphook. Address 13ᵗʰ D.L.I., Bramshott, Hants. Since returning I have been rather hustled – it is bad enough being transferred to a strange company, but, in addition, owing to the absence of the junior captain, I found myself temporarily second in command – then a further shock last night; the company-commander, an excellent man, is suddenly

summoned to join the Expeditionary Force in France at 24 hours'
notice, so now I am in charge of 240 men, scarcely one of whom
I know by sight! This is likely to continue for perhaps a fortnight,
and involves immensely complicated accounts and considerably
more responsibility than is good for any one at such short notice.

However, I hope to pull through!"

Bramshott, 30ᵗʰ May, 1915.
"We arrived here safely (by train) on Sunday. This camp holds
two Brigades, 68ᵗʰ and 69ᵗʰ, and is situated just south of the
Portsmouth Road, 1 ½ miles west of Hindhead; it's a splendid
position – the officers' quarters are ¼ mile from the road and
overlooking the valley along which the railway runs. Mrs. B.'s
cottage is about 1 ½ miles off, and I have been there twice for
bath and dinner. I think the huts quite a success. It is like being
under canvas without some of the discomforts. The men have
straw mattresses and plenty of elbow room. The whole business is
more like active service than anything we have done yet. We have
eschewed the caterer's mess for officers and draw the ordinary
army rations; these are supplemented by groceries etc., and cooked
(very excellently) by our own soldier cooks. It seems curious that
we have not done this before, because, besides saving expense, we
are certainly feeding better than at Bullswater, or even Aldershot.

I am getting into the way of my new job. The business part
gives me most bother, but at present the accounts are simplified
by the fact that all the Company Books are in the hands of the
Paymaster, so that one cannot attempt to make out a balance.

No sign of rifles or ammunition yet, but there is a general
feeling that the days of our training are numbered and I rather
expect to make a sea voyage before arriving at my 30ᵗʰ birthday."

The following section of the Diary, with the exception of the first few lines written at Bramshott, was written in France. George was in the neighborhood of Armentieres till February; then his Division, after spending a short time at Hazebrucke, Marles-les-Mines and Fresnicourt in succession, was at the beginning of March ordered south in order to take over the line at Souchez neighborhood until the Division was again moved south to take part in the battle of the Somme, as outlined in his July letters. A.K.B.

August, 1915.

I have not kept any sort of record of things for six months and more; our existence has been far too monotonous, and at times one has been tempted to believe that we were not really meant for active service at all. But now it seems we are actually going to be used. There is not much to be said about the intervening period, and in any case it would be stale news; suffice it that by the middle of July we had completed our musketry course, and were more or less fully trained and equipped.

Bramshott, 25ᵗʰ August, 1915.

"We are off this evening, but I don't know from what port."

There had been some changes of personnel; Colonel Ashby left us some weeks ago (superannuated) and Major Biddulph is now C.O. There was also some inter-company exchange of officers, and I myself was transferred to A Company in May (after promotion to full lieutenant). For nearly a month in the absence of the seniors, I was Acting Company Commander, and am now the senior subaltern, in charge of No. 2 Platoon.

At the time of writing we had been stationed for three months in huts at Bramshott, near Haslemere. The first sign of possible business to come was on Thursday, August 19th, when the King came down to review the 23rd Division. Very short notice was given, and several officers who were on leave at the time had to be recalled by wire.

The inspection was rather more interesting than most; the Division had its rendezvous in open country about half way between Guildford and Haslemere – an ideal spot for the purpose. It was certainly a fine sight, and the moment when the King, at the head of his train, galloped into sight through a defile in the hills, was quite thrilling.

However, no one suspected any immediate developments, and the interrupted leave was resumed, but it was not destined to be more than a one-day excursion, for on the evening of Friday, August 20th, orders came that we were to mobilize.

Of course everyone was very excited; one felt that a little of the real thing, after months and months of sham and boredom, must be a change for the good. The camp was in uproar most of the night – quite in the old Bullswater style.

However, the actual process of mobilizing, apart from the uncertainty of our movements and destination, was not very exciting. As far as I was concerned, it consisted chiefly in making out lists of kit deficiencies and 'pinching' as much as possible from the quartermaster. We were not able to get away, as the authorities pretended that we might be starting any moment.

Eventually we got our orders to march on Wednesday, August 25th.

We knew that we were bound for France, but our exact route was not stated, and the censor will not allow me to say anything about it.

We had a perfect crossing, by night – getting on and off the boat was a matter of minutes only, and it was impossible to believe it was the work of the W.D. A single destroyer acted as escort, and no incident occurred.

We landed in the early morning and marched a few miles to camp, where we rested for the remainder of the day. In the middle of the night we moved on again, marched a few miles to a railway and then sat down and waited for a train to take us to the front. The transport arrangements at this point were defective, as we had to wait about two hours by the side of the line, during which time some fifty trains must have passed us, mostly empty and returning to the base. At length ours turned up – three first class compartments for the officers and cattle trucks for the men, 40 in each. A rumour got about that we going straight up to the front, but after a few hours' journey the train pulled up at a small wayside station; here we got out, a French interpreter took charge, and we marched five very hot and dusty miles to _____, a village where billets were provided for us.

Here we remained for over a week – about 40 miles from the firing line – and were fairly comfortable, the officers being quartered in farm houses and the men in adjacent barns. We could hear the big guns quite distinctly most days. During this period we went on training exactly as in England, and quickly relapsed into our dull and monotonous habits; in fact things seemed much quieter than at Bramshott, and the only sense of war was provided by the heavy traffic and scorching dispatch riders on the main road which led direct to the British Headquarters.

The country here is not unlike England – and the people also. It is possible that they have been unconsciously influenced by the English invasion, and they have certainly been tremendously sobered by the war. This was very striking, in contrast with our people at home; I have never heard a soul speak either jestingly or excitedly about future prospects; the French people are certainly going to stand firm. As for the French soldiers, they were not to be seen. The English army fills the whole countryside, and has become part of the normal life – relations with the inhabitants are excellent, but of course there is none of the enthusiasm such as would have greeted us a year ago.

One of my daily tasks is the censoring of men's letters; I have to read them, sign the envelope and then they are franked by the Orderly Room. This becomes irksome after a time, but it is also of great human interest. I don't think I ever realised the difference between married and single! As to what they say, of course there is very little news – they all seem astonished at finding they can't understand the language, and they all complain because they can't get English cigarettes. Any present of these will be welcome, but they must be "Woodbines" (1d. a packet).

On Monday, September 6th, we moved on – a long march of over 20 miles. For various reasons this exhausted us very much – in fact far more than anything we had ever done, the chief causes being (1) the heat, (2) cobbled roads, (3) weight of packs. As regards the last, I ought to say that out here the men carry all their belongings on their backs, and as we have not yet learnt what to throw away the weight is tremendous. At least one in ten fell out, and one can hardly blame them. The weather has been very hot almost all the time so far. On arrival at our destination we put up billets for the night.

Next day, September 7th, we marched again – only 15 miles this time, but weather hotter still. Nearly half the Brigade fell out on the way!

This march brought us within five or six miles of the front, and we could hear the rifles cracking quite distinctly. Billets of the usual country type, i.e. farms and barns.

Next day, September 8th, we were inspected by the General Commanding our Army Corps, who kindly informed us what we were supposed to be doing, a subject about which we had all been very much in the dark.

He said that we were to go up into the trenches by platoons, for "instructional purposes," 24 hours at a stretch, being attached to the unity actually on duty there. We were to do this for four days (two days in and two out), and then retire into safety for further training and finally take up our own positions in the line, in perhaps two or three weeks' time.

Sept. 11th.

"Herewith first installment of news. In future I will try and write it up to date every few days. We have been in the trenches for 24 hours, and I will tell you about it in my next. Am quite well.

Thanks for letter, also papers: please don't trouble about the latter, as we get them regularly. We have not really settled down properly to the life here yet, and I don't really know what I want sent out. I am short of several things at present, and am simply waiting for the first opportunity of getting into a town to replenish."

September 18th.

We have been in the fire-trenches 3 times – twenty-four hours at a stretch. This was just a preliminary canter, and none of us had any real responsibility, merely assisting those already in possession. Naturally enough we were not put into any of the dangerous sections, but it may be of some interest to describe what a normal day on a quiet part of the front is like. The first day we started from a point some miles in rear, and timed our march so as to get up after dark. As we got nearer and twilight set in, the artillery noises grew more and more insistent; ours seemed to predominate, and every gun within miles had its turn at the evening "hate", which is an affair of regular occurrence. As night set in the artillery fire ceased, but the rifles went on cracking continuously with every now and then a splutter of machine guns. We reached the entrance of the communication trench safely; it is about 600 yards long, and so our guide lost his way several times, we spent a long time in it; stray bullets were now flying all about, and the explosive sound they cause as they pass overhead was new to most of us; the depth of the trench, however made things quite safe. At last we filed into the fire-trench, and immediately opposite the entrance I found, to my astonishment, a little wooded shanty, and the officers of the company having dinner; so at the moment when I felt braced up for a vigorous onslaught on the Hun, I was hauled off to roast beef and beer, while a sergeant posted my men.

Later on I went along the line with the officer of the watch. Every minute or so a flare went up, and then the enemy position was plainly visible about a quarter of a mile away (the trenches here are really breastworks, built up high with sandbags).

The sentries and snipers on either side exchange compliments pretty frequently, though there is rarely anything to fire at (I have not seen a German yet). In the trench, one is perfectly safe from them; it is the working parties behind who are worried by the stray bullets. And so it goes on all night, and every night; occasionally a machine-gun gets on to a target (real or imaginary) and there is half-a-minute's concentrated fury, after which comparative peace again.

It is extraordinary how soon one gets accustomed to this entire rattle. I slept excellently each night I was in, and as I was not on any special duty I was able to get a decent amount of rest.

By day there is very little rifle fire, the sentries are fewer in number and work by periscope; the German snipers make it dangerous for anyone to expose his head above the parapet by day for more than just a second or two (even at 500 yards). In this respect they are all over us – and in fact we are still well behind the Hun in all the tricks of trench warfare; as regards machine guns we have pretty well caught up, and our artillery distinctly has superiority.

As far as my platoon was concerned, we had a very quiet time each day we were up; only one shell fell anywhere near us and we have not had anyone hit. Others have not been quite so lucky; one platoon was caught by a machine gun on its way home the very first night (presumably through the guide's fault), and had five wounded. Another lot narrowly escaped destruction by a mine explosion, but the battalion has lost less than twelve wounded altogether and none killed.

So much for our period of instruction; we are now in divisional reserve four miles behind the front, and expect to take up duty in our own allotted section in about a week's time. There is not much excitement here, but we hear the artillery at work practically all the time; usually it is simply a gun or two trying to annoy somebody, but occasionally there is a concentrated "strafe" for half-an-hour or so, and then we all sit up and wonder if someone is trying to attack; and of course there is always a chance that we may be shelled ourselves. But no one minds that.

Sept. 20th.

"And so Zepps have been to London at last; such things seem small out here, where the sounds of destruction are audible all day and night. It is extraordinary how long one may manage to keep out of it. I have been three times up to the front line, and so far have seen only one shell burst, and have not seen a single (a) dead man, (b) wounded man, (c) German, (d) gun.

I have sent the 'General'* two installments of news; will you please ask him to see that nothing I send home gets into print. The authorities are getting nasty about it, even when the matter is harmless."

[* His Father]

Sept. 29th.

Just a line to let you know all is well. You will know all about the latest developments. We have been in reserve all the time, and have seen nothing yet, but plenty of moving about."

<u>Saturday, October 2nd</u>.

Although big things have been happening, I have very little news to give of the last ten days. We had a very quiet week in our bivouac, the time being occupied partly by work on reserve trenches, partly by the ordinary training (so called), of which everyone is heartily sick. In fact the men now regard the trenches as rest, and billet life as a tiresome drudgery.

Then on Saturday, September 25th, as everyone knows, came the big push, preceded by a two days' bombardment, more or less continuous and at times extremely violent. We had known about this for some days before, but all details were kept dark, and even now we know very little more than has appeared in the papers.

As far as our share went, it consisted in being marched hurriedly about between the bivouac and a certain town where we are now billeted (7 miles) – apparently we were being used as corps (not divisional) reserve – ready to assist wherever required.

So far we have not been needed, and for the last few days things have been very quiet along this front; we can only guess at what is happening elsewhere, and what is going to happen.

———————————————————

Oct. 7th, 1915.

"We have moved again, and are now in reserve to our own Brigade. We relieve the 12th D.L.I. shortly, and shall be in the trenches for perhaps a week. Things very quiet – in fact much quieter than when we first came out. There seems to be a temporary shortage (or economy) of shells on both sides, which is probably inevitable after the deluge of September 23-45."

Oct. 21st.

"I'm afraid I have not written home for ages, but we have been busy. We have just completed our second turn in the trenches, and in between I went on a course of machine gunnery.

We had a quiet time, and good weather, which is the chief blessing. What a place would be like after a couple of days' rain I can't imagine."

Oct. 22nd.

"We have now completed our second turn in the trenches – casualties small, but including two officers. The weather has been marvelously kind to us – it never seems to rain at all except when we are in billets. Somewhat cold at night.

We are now in Brigade Reserve for a few days, and hope to be more or less unmolested (by the authorities, I mean)."

October 28th.

Since my last communique (!) we have had two turns in the trenches and a short rest between; we are now in the billets (fairly comfortable), and it is quite uncertain what we are going to do next, or when.

I will try and give some idea of what daily life in the trenches (i.e., ours) is like, so far as is permissible.

In the first place, there are practically no real trenches at all in this part of the country; we are here practically at sea level, and the spade finds water almost at once, hence protection has to be given with barricades of earth and sandbags. The front barricade is continuous all along the line, and behind it – for protection against shell fire – is a conglomeration of passages and cross walls; the geography of these is worthy of the maze at Hampton Court, and in striking contrast to the neat regularity of trenches built for training purposes. (Incidentally I had never seen a breastwork before coming over here.)

All these walls have now been standing for nearly a year, they are in need of constant repair; there are enough rats in them to eat up the whole British Army. One advantage of breastworks over trenches is that one can walk behind them to a depth of 25 yards without fear of being hit by bullets.

As to our routine – by night we have a good number of sentries watching the front; these are relieved periodically, and the spare men are kept in readiness for emergencies.

By day there are, of course, fewer sentries, and they work entirely by periscope.

Sentry duty is always taken very seriously, no matter how easy the conditions, and a sentry found asleep is automatically sent up for a court-martial.

The difference between night and day conditions is very great. By night, although spasmodic firing is always going on, we have not had a single man hit, and one could quite happily eat one's supper on the parapet, provided one retired below for one's smoke!

On the other hand, by day it is usually (though not always) extremely dangerous to expose even the top part of one's head for more than two or three seconds. A German sniper, even at 400 yards, can make pretty good practice at a six inch target, and we have already lost an officer and one or two men in that way. Moreover they frequently crawl out at night and take up a position from which by day they can pot away at our parapet without fear of detection. Of course it is the telescopic rifle that does it, and it is curious that the authorities do not think that it is worthwhile to put us on equality in this respect. But in reality this sniping business is more of a nuisance than a danger, and it is quite unnecessary for anyone to expose himself by day, and by night the sniper can do nothing much.

So much for sentry duty – and there is not much else, as far as routine goes. The rest of the men's time is divided up between (a) rest (chiefly by day); (b) carrying supplies up from the dumping ground (which can be done at any time due to the communications trenches); (c) repairs (chiefly by night).

As to the Officers, our duties are similar; we take it in turn to be "officers of the watch", which means constantly visiting the sentries, noting incidents of interest, and generally keeping a lookout; at other times there are occasional odd jobs, but otherwise one can rest, and I usually managed to get six hours' sleep out of twenty-four, which is pretty good – boots always on, when asleep. There is a plentiful supply of dug-outs, and one can be quite comfortable. One dug-out serves as a mess-room for the officers of the company, and we have no difficulty in getting up provisions; the men also get their ordinary rations, and so long as the weather is fine (which, curiously enough, has been the case with us so far) all is well.

So much for daily routine. Now for a few incidents, chiefly connected with sorties into "No Man's Land."

1. On one occasion we decided to attempt "reprisals" against the German snipers; two men detailed to go out before daybreak, take up a position, annoy the enemy as much as possible during the day, and return as soon as it got dark. We waited anxiously for their return, and eventually Headquarters' phoned up that we were to send out a strong search party (of which more anon). This was not successful, and we had given the men up, but in the middle of the next morning, to our great joy, they turned up, having been in the open for 36 hours.

2. It appears they crawled close up to the enemy parapet, and accounted for two men during the day; when it got dark they tried to get back, but were cut off (or thought they were) by patrols; so they lay still all night. Next morning they managed to crawl into a ditch, which fortunately led almost up to our lines. For this exploit they are probably getting a DCM.

3. The Rescue Party – This was a very tame affair. I was put in charge, and perhaps did not take it very seriously, for it seemed to me that we had a very small chance at night time of finding men, presumably wounded, without having some definite idea of where to look for them. However, it was a novel experience, and probably did us good:

We filed out (about 16 strong) by the usual exit, myself in rear, according to instructions. When first clear of our wire everyone suddenly lay down, and at the same time I heard a noise in a tree just to our left. Feeling sure that it was a man I got hold of a bomber, and together we stalked up to the tree. I then challenged softly, and no answer being given, the bomber hurled his bomb, which went off in great style. It struck me afterwards that it was foolish to give ourselves away so early in the proceedings, but I am narrating this as an example of how not to conduct a patrol. After satisfying ourselves that there had never been anyone there, we rejoined the others, and I passed up the order to advance. After ten yards crawling everyone lay down again, and this went on for about half-an-hour. By this time I was getting tired – also wet, and as we only had a limited time at our disposal, I decided to go up to the front – instructions notwithstanding – and push on a bit faster; our procedure, moreover, was beginning to strike me as rather ludicrous, as we were strong enough to frighten away any patrol likely to be out. So we went forward about 150 yards without meeting anything, and as time was getting short, I decided to circle round and return by a different route to our starting point. By this time everyone had acquired a certain degree of confidence – seeing that not one shot had been fired in our direction – and the last part of our journey was carried out at a brisk walk, and without any attempt at concealment. And so ended my first and (at present) only attempt at night patrolling. Casualties nil. Results, ditto, except some experience and amusement.

I think that this is all I have to say about our trench experiences to date. Next time we shall probably find out what it is like in wet weather.

P.S. – Anyone reading the above must see that none of it gets into print.

[This is the end of the Diary.]

Nov. 2nd.

"I hope you have my last budget.

We have now had a full fortnight's 'rest,' and for myself it has been almost literally rest. I have done practically nothing but eat, sleep and play chess! (No chess in the trenches, because one is glad to sleep all one's spare time.) There is nothing else to do here – no places to go to, the most frightfully dull country imaginable, and any amount of rain. We are shortly going to start another round..????????

I had a splendid parcel from D., rather extravagantly large… We have a Company Mess of five officers, and all contribute. We also get the ordinary soldier's ration, and are usually able to buy milk, butter etc., so we are not badly off."

Nov. 14th.

"Just a line to let you know my present movements. I have just been sent on an eight days' course of instruction in bombs – they are gradually training all men and officers. So for the present I am away from the battalion, and away from all danger, except our own clumsiness in bomb-chucking. I am billeted with two other officers in a nice farm house – with beds (!) - and our discomfort is the MUD. This word may be said to pretty well to describe our existence – it is bad enough here and everywhere, but in the trenches there is nothing else (even the water is really liquid mud). My trench coat now has an extra thickness from top to bottom. In short we are getting some idea of what a winter campaign really is.

You will be very sorry to hear that Brown has been killed; he was out in front of the parapet one night, and seems to have lost his way and fallen into an ambuscade; the man with him managed to carry him back – a wonderful performance, as he was under fire most of the way and had to crawl – and he died on the way to the dressing station.

P.S. - We get the daily papers regularly, but an occasional magazine (Punch, Strand, etc.) would be welcome – novels are not much used."

Nov. 22nd.

"I am afraid I have left you some time without a letter, but there has been nothing to write about. I suppose you got my letter from the Bombing School. I am now back with the Battalion (in billets). We go into trenches again some day this week - weather very cold, but we all prefer the frost to wet.

By the way, we are just starting leave – you must let me know when you would like me to come – my turn will normally come about the New Year, but it will be easy to arrange very long beforehand."

Nov. 28ᵗʰ.

"We have just completed another turn in trenches – hard frost all the time, but on the whole we rather enjoyed it. I'm afraid the men found it difficult to sleep because of the cold, but we are managing to keep clear of frostbite and other trench ills. We had a very quiet time, and I think it was the first tour of duty in which the company had no casualties at all.

I hope the N.E.R. Battalion will have luck – it is rather thankless work* out here, and our Pioneer Battalion has certainly had more than its share of artillery and machine gun fire.

Many thanks for the books, which I hope to read in time."
[* Meaning obviously the work of the Pioneer Battalion. The Battalion here referred to is a Pioneer Battalion raised by the North Eastern Railway Company (17ᵗʰ Northumberland Fusiliers)].

Dec. 9ᵗʰ, 1915.

"I think I have been getting things pretty regularly, except perhaps the last week or so. I have been away four days, and when that happens our battalion postal arrangements are apt to break down; if anything has gone astray, I shall probably get it about Christmas. The reason for my absence is that I got a chill, and went to a convalescent home instead of the trenches. Am all right again now. I'm afraid I have not sent you any news for a long time, but our existence is pretty monotonous – in fact it is just bare existence, and nothing besides. I never know what the day of week is, even Sunday.. . . . .

I read 'Aunt Sarah' in bed, and enjoyed it, though I don't think the author has been to the front and the chronology is poor;

there was no trench warfare in August, 1914, and a new recruit would hardly be home wounded at the time of Ypres (No. 1)!

Shall be glad of literature occasionally, if not too bulky.

. . . . .

I didn't send you an account of the bomb school, because it was rather a farce as far as I was concerned, being really a course for men, not officers. However, I threw a few bombs with fair accuracy (20-25 yards). It is an easy subject to master, especially now that we have at last got the thing standardized – there is practically only one kind used now, and it is a very neat weapon. In a battle the chief difficulty is to organize your parties, and keep them supplied the whole time; at the present stage of things, of course, we practically never use bombs.

I can probably arrange to take my leave on January 22, so that if you can fix a date in that week, all will be well."

Dec. 13ᵗʰ. (in trenches)
"Please tell the General* not to bother about the armour-plating, as it is not the sort of thing which can be done privately.

No special news – the wet is terrific - one wades to one's bed, and eats one's dinner with water over the ankles, but with waders and four changes of socks I keep fairly dry."
[* His Father]

Dec. 19ᵗʰ.
"Did you see about our V.C.? Account enclosed. The first in our Division, and the first in the D.L.I. for many years."

1916

Feb. 5th, 1916.

"I have been sent on a course of signaling (i.e., telephone, buzzer, etc.). It promises to be interesting, and at any rate novel. To-day (the first) I have already learnt to make a clove-hitch knot, mend breaks in cable, Morse alphabet (more or less), and how to run a line across country – all of which seems very remote from the war, though of course it is part of a very important department.

One result is that probably we shall be in the Corps reserve by the time this is through, in which case I may see no more of the trenches until the end of March!

I had an uneventful journey back, except for fog in the channel; the day in Boulogne was pleasant, but much more expensive than the Cecil.

I enjoyed my leave very much, and am very glad that everything connected with the ceremony* went off so well." [*the wedding of his father and Dorothea 'Dolly' Ionides on January 26th. WS]

Feb. 25th.

"The course finishes on Sunday, and after that my address will be as before. It is quite uncertain what we shall be doing, but I think it very probable that the 'rest' will be (or has been) cancelled. Very severe weather the last few days, but quite pleasant for us here.

The course has been quite enjoyable; it is the first time I have ever taken the slightest interest in anything scientific, and I am beginning to feel quite a practical man. Besides telephone and 'buzzing', we have done work at laying cables, mending ditto, also signaling with flag, helio, lamp, etc."

Feb. 28th.

"I rejoined the Battalion yesterday; at the present moment we are in Corps 'rest', some miles behind the line. Normally we should be here a month, but from the unsettled look of things it hardly seems likely we shall get our full time. The Verdun business is tremendous; so far (Sunday's paper) results seem satisfactory."

March 4th.

"I hope you got my last, saying that I had rejoined the battalion – actually before posting it we got orders to move, and were hurried off by train to an entirely different part of the front – or rather not the front, but a town about 15 miles behind it. Our present function is obscure; apparently we are no longer general reserve, because we (i.e., our Division) have been definitely attached to a new Army Corps. The idea at present seems to be that we are shortly going to take over a definite section of trenches in this neighborhood.

Whatever happens, thank goodness, we have got away from the plain. This is a hilly, mining neighborhood, very like the north of England. We are billeted (very comfortably) in a large mining village, so the men are thoroughly at home; in fact the last few days have been about the best rest we ever had.

I told my N.C.O.'s yesterday that I thought the next two months would see a definite decision (though not the actual finish). It seems arithmetically possible for the Germans to make one more offensive on the scale of Verdun, but I think that is their limit, and when that is over we shall be through with the winter, and a combined offensive on all fronts will be practicable. At present we are having a renewal of bad weather – heavy snow today.

March 5th.

"We are moving to-morrow; the Division is taking up a new sector of line. We shall be in the reserve at first, and go into trenches in about a weeks' time. It is supposed to be rather a hot neighborhood, but it is certainly our turn to do something."

March 15th.

"We have been billeted in a pleasant village here for the last week, and plans have slightly altered again. We are going to take over trenches (in a day or two) a few miles off where we expected to go. I hear they are very good trenches. No other news. The last of the snow has disappeared, and we are having lovely weather."

March 22nd.

"We have just returned from our first turn in trenches, and it was quite enjoyable – trenches dug down deep in chalk soil, and no water – much safer than what we have been accustomed to.

Things are moderately lively; we are not likely to have serious trouble here, though there is historic ground on either side. Weather has been fine and warm.

We have got a new Brigadier (our fourth). You will be interested to know his name, i.e., Page Croft, M.P.; you sent me a newspaper report of one of his speeches in the House – he seems a good man.

I have just seen in 'The Times' that poor old Victor B.-K. is missing."

March 27th.

"We are in the trenches again, and the weather is compelling us to resort to rubber boots again, though we are not likely to get water more than ankle-deep in this soil.

Nothing else to report - 'situation normal,' in the words of the daily bulletin."

March 31st.

"We are at present in reserve, after another tour in trenches – having a pretty good time – lovely spring weather at present, different from what you seem to be getting. Future movements uncertain, but I don't fancy the present quiescence will continue long, considering what is happening in Russia and Italy. By the way, I think you are wrong about the British line; I have certainly seen it stated in the papers that it is now continuous from Ypres to the Somme, in which case it must have been pretty well doubled since Christmas.

Have heard from Colonel B.-K., Victor's fate is uncertain, but it seems probable that he was hit (or machine damaged) at a great height, and fell nose down."

April 16th.

"Just a line to let you know we are out of trenches, and are expecting, if things remain normal, to have a fairly long rest (?)."

Easter Day.

"All going well, save the wet weather, which however now shows signs of improving. Except for occasional working-parties we are having a very easy week, in good billets. After this we shall probably go further back and have a week's maneuvers, which will be a change. I shall be glad of a few books. If D. sent 'Count Bunker,' please thank her from me very much, and ask for more. Meanwhile there is a good deal of comic relief to be derived from home and American news – in Parliament the antics of that amazing idiot, P. Billing, M.P.

The recruiting 'crisis' is too stupid for words. One can't understand how it ever arose, and Asquith is much to blame for allowing it. On the other hand the conscription campaign has been equally muddled, owing to the difference between those who want it for the sake of getting the numbers, and those who want it because they like it – like Harmsworth. Naturally the latter sort are objects of suspicion."

April 28th.
"Summer has descended on us in some style, and the clothing problem has suddenly taken a new turn.

We have moved further back and are now billeted in pleasant country – fairly complete rest, of which the M.O. has taken advantage to inoculate us all again.

It is difficult to realise that we have really come through a winter campaign; I suppose one can consider it satisfactory as a test of physical fitness, though we have certainly been lucky, the worst weather nearly always having found us in billets. We have been equally fortunate as regards the attentions of the enemy, and there must be few battalions with seven months' trench experience whose total killed amount to less than fifty."

May 9th.
"We are having a good long rest, i.e., away from trenches, at present in a remote country village, full of orchards, birds and

streams – maneuvers all the morning, which at least help to keep one healthy. Shall probably keep at the same sort of thing for a week or so.

The General* seems very pessimistic about the Government! I am sorry he goes so far as to support the 'Ginger' group. I would rather be governed by Harry Tate than by Carson, and L.G. seems to be playing to the gallery at least as much as at Limehouse."

[* Ed. his Father]

Sunday, May 28th .

"As you probably guessed, we have been in the trenches again – rather sooner than I expected. You may also have imagined that things have been more lively than usual; as a matter of fact, on our immediate front things have been quiet; casualties below normal, which is astonishing considering what was going on within a mile or two of us, i.e., the battle of _____ , which presumably you have read about. It was a pretty intense business, as far as artillery was concerned, and a new experience for us, for we practically overlook the ground in dispute.

I am expecting leave shortly, so will reserve further account.

[AKB: 'George was home on leave from June 1st to June 8th and was in excellent health and spirits.']

June 13th.

"As I expected, we are now out of the trenches, and are apparently going to have another spell of training – there are many rumors as to our next destination, but no one really knows anything.

My journey back took two whole days, including a night at Boulogne.

No news whatever and weather awfully bad."

June 17th.

"Many thanks for watch-guard, which suits excellently.

I think I told you we are in rest again – that being so I have of course no news; the only things of interest lies in future movements, of which I know very little and must say less.

Weather improving by degrees."

June 26th:

"Not much news, except that we have moved again (and a good long way) and are now in reserve to a different part of the line. Please thank D. for sunshade."

July 2nd, 1916.

"By the time you get this the papers will be full of what is going on here. At present we know very little, except that the much-advertised offensive has started and made some progress.

We are at present acting as a reserve at what seems about the centre of the main push. We have been moving up by easy stages – billets each night – and are at present about 12 miles from the line. Everything seems very quiet, and we can scarcely hear the guns, a phenomenon I completely fail to understand. It is impossible to say how soon we shall come into action, but we are bound to do sooner or later, unless our plans go wrong altogether. Fortunately the weather has turned fine, and seems likely to remain so. I will try to get some field postcards to correspond with, as they will reach you quicker than letters."

July 3rd.

"Last night we moved up a bit further, and are now within an easy march of the front. When we got to our destination (at about midnight) we found our billets full of prisoners. So the whole brigade was turned into a field and ordered to bivouac. This consists chiefly of lying down on a waterproof sheet. The men have no overcoats! I have my Reading mackintosh, and managed three hours' sleep – not bad with the temperature little above 40 degrees. There is no mistake about the bombardment now. We get very scanty news from the front, and have seen no papers since the show began. Weather still fine, and pleasantly warm in the daytime."

July 5th.

"I'm afraid these letters will reach you very late – the mail is much interrupted and I can't get any field cards. We moved here on the 3rd, about five miles behind the line, bivouacs, but we fortunately have some tarpaulin tents. Last night we were ordered forward, but after we had marched about three miles, orders were cancelled, and we returned to our new starting point. At least we had the satisfaction of seeing a few (!) of the British guns in action.

We still get very little news – on the whole things seem to be going well, if rather slowly. The French have done brilliantly, as usual, but they probably had the easier job."

July 7th.

"Just a line to say all well at present. No time for more."

July 12th. !!!

"In brief my news is: (1) We have been up to the front for a few days. (2) Have done no actual fighting. (3) Are back in rest for a few days.

I am not going to attempt any description – of course the conditions are utterly different from anything we are accustomed to. The ordinary placid routine of trench warfare exists no longer: one has a general sense of confusion, and shells fly about day and night. Add to that the wet weather, and mud that requires all one's energy to wade through, and you will have some idea.

All the same it is obvious that our hardships are child's play compared to what the German's are undergoing – our guns give them no rest whatever.

Am quite well."

[AKB: 'George's 31st Birthday.']

July 14th.

"Very many thanks for birthday present and letter. Also your last food parcel was very opportune, as we were just starting off for the great battle.

We were up in the line for a few days, which seemed like so many weeks – but on the whole we had extraordinary luck. We never came into actual close contact with the Hun, but on the other hand we never knew exactly where he was, and often were quite vague as to where we were ourselves. Our worst enemy was the weather, which for two days was really bad. It sounds incredible, but it is true that the mud was far worse than in any of the Armentieres trenches throughout the winter. This is chiefly due to the soil.

We are now back, billeted in a certain town.

I lost practically all my portable equipment, and finally came out with 1 revolver (unused), 1 map, and 1 flask (empty!)."

July 22nd.
"We are out again for a rest, and I hope a good one this time. The last was not much use, as we were still within the shell area, and the concussion of our own guns brought portions of the rickety cottages down every time.

We are now well back, and the noise of battle is only just audible.

We have now had two turns in the battle line (more or less) and the second was better than the first – at any rate as far as weather was concerned. I will try and write some account of our doings and post it to you at some future time, when the contents will no longer be anathema to the censor.

We have again been lucky (i.e., our battalion); twice we have been within an ace of being shoved into a desperate venture, but as a fact we have not attacked at all yet – consequentially practically all our casualties are from the shell fire, and, as you know, only a very small proportion of these are fatal, or even serious.

I have had charge of my company for the last fortnight, since the O.C. was wounded. I was standing beside him at the time, and I think the one shell laid out about a dozen (a very rare event). In fact I must have been the only man in the neighborhood untouched, and suffered no after effects except slight deafness in one ear, which has now passed off.

I tell you this to cheer you up!!"

July 27ᵗʰ, 1916.

"In the trenches again, at present in support – plans uncertain. No trouble at present yet except intermittent shrapnel. This morning a small fragment hit me in the back, and made a slight scratch, which I had dressed. This is merely to warn you in case you should see my name in the casualty list! They have a way of reporting even the slightest cases."

[AKB: 'This letter was not received till August 4. On July 31 a telegram was received from the War Office reporting George as "wounded."']

July 29ᵗʰ.

"Back in the billets again after two nights only in the line – nothing much doing. Probably going up again soon. Thanks for the letter!"

[AKB: 'This letter was received on August 2.']

Official War Battalion Dispatch - 5th August, 1916:

0005 hours. Ordered OC 'C' Coy 10 NF to proceed up Gloster Alley and relieve Lt Butterworth in Butterworth Trench.

0010 hours. Ordered Lt Butterworth (EB 169) as follows: *"proceed round the loop with your company and form up there for the attack. Take bombs and tools. Move as quickly as possible".*

Note: Lt. Butterworth was prevented from carrying out order by own artillery fire.

0040 hours. Brigadier on advice of Brigadier Major decided not to carry out another attack.

0147 hours. Capt Lincoln OC 'C' Coy 10 NF telephoned *"being heavily shelled by our artillery".*

0148 hours. Lt Beale 10th West Ridings phoned he had taken up position in OG2 to which he had been ordered by Brigadier after it had been evacuated by 'C' Coy 10 NF.

0207 hours. Lt Davenport found our guns were shelling his platoon on left of Butterworth Trench.

0220 hours. Lt Clark found that Lt Target was killed and most of his men, that he was collecting men of 'D' Coy under 2nd Lts Sant and Atkinson and sending them up Munster Alley.

0253 hours. Sent following message to Lt Butterworth at 'B' Coy *"Send a strong bombing platoon up Munster Alley to our block".*

Note: Owing to our artillery shelling on the front line, Lt Butterworth cannot have received this message till after 0345 hrs.

0333 hours. Asked Lt Clark to supply 2nd Lt Batty with 10 men to go round to W entrance of Torr Trench and try and get trench mortar from Anzacs.

0340 hours. Received following from Lt Clark *"We must have reinforcements up at once. The platoon of 'A' Coy has not turned up and the men I have got there are being kept there with revolvers".*

0341 hours. Gave 2nd Lt Batty message for Butterworth to reinforce Munster Alley with one platoon at once.

0419 hours. Forward Observation reported that our party in Munster Alley was being heavily bombed but that we were apparently holding our own.

0443 hours. The Brigadier sent 25 men from another unit to relieve Butterworth.

0445 hours. Lt Butterworth killed.

Casualties 5th August:

Lt G S Kaye-Butterworth, Lt N A Target killed;
2nd Lts Rees and Batty wounded.
Other ranks: 4 killed, 18 wounded, 3 shell shock, 5 missing.

A.K. Butterworth:

'I do not know whether George carried out his intentions of trying to put on paper what he saw of the battle of the Somme up to the 22nd July, for no papers were sent home with his kit. No one could guess from his July letters that the 13th Durham Light Infantry were engaged in the great battle more or less continuously throughout the month. One is able to gain some general idea of the operations in which the battalion took part from "Twenty-two months under Fire," by General Page Croft, then in command of the 68th Brigade. From the account there given it appears that on July 3rd the brigade, which in the latter part of June had been sent south to Millencourt, moved up to Albert, where they lay in trenches one night. On the 4th the brigade moved up to Becourt Wood. From the 7th to the 10th, the British having by that time captured the first system of German trenches, the brigade took part in what General Page Croft describes as "the second series of operations," of which an attack on Contalmaison formed part. The attack began on the morning of the 7th, but apparently it was not till the 9th that the two battalions of the Durham's succeeded in capturing Bailiff Wood, one of the main objectives of the brigade, which was situated just to the west of the village. The village itself was secured on the 10th by another brigade after stiff hand-to-hand fighting, and on the 11th the 68th were relieved and marched back to Albert. Colonel Wilkinson wrote that he brought forward George's name "for his work during the period 7th to the 10th July," and General Page Croft, referring no doubt to the same time, that "he recommended him for an earlier action" (i.e. earlier than the attack on Munster Alley) "near Contalmaison for the

Military Cross." It must have been at this time that George's Company Commander was wounded, leaving him in command of the Company until his death.

The brigade was then lent to another Division which had lost heavily, and on the 15th marched eastwards again to the Usna-Tara line of trenches, the objective this time being Pozieres. On the night of the 17th the Durham's made an unsuccessful attack on a German trench, in which one Company lost every officer, and, as a frontal attack on the village seemed impracticable, the 18th and 19th were occupied in consolidating some 1,600 yards of new trench within 250 yards of the enemy. The brigade was then relieved by the Australians and reached Albert at 4am on the 20th, and on the same day marched back 10 miles to rejoin its own Division which had been resting near Frenvillers. In this set of operations Colonel Wilkinson says that George "got his men to accomplish a good bit of work in linking up the front line," this earning him, apparently, the Military Cross for the second time.

At Frenvillers the brigade was reorganised and replenished by drafts, but the 'rest' was very short – only five days – for on the 26th they marched from Frenvillers through Contalmaison and joined the right of the Australian Division about half a mile east of Pozieres, the trench called Munster Alley being the dividing line between the two Divisions. This trench, which ran at right angles to the British front straight into the enemy's line, had been repeatedly attacked without success. The day after their arrival (on which George reported that he was slightly wounded) the brigade made a fresh attack and secured 70 yards of the trench. This position was consolidated, and on the night of the 28th they marched back, two battalions to the Sausage Valley and two to Albert.

George's last letter is dated the 29th and must have been written during the short period of rest which intervened before the brigade was sent to the front line for the fourth, and last, time on the 1st August. It must, I think, have been then that "Butterworth Trench" was dug, three days before the successful attack upon Munster Alley by the 13th D.L.I. It seems that two simultaneous attacks upon Munster Alley were made on the 4th, one by a bombing party, under George's command, up the trench, and the other an attack "over the top" from the loop in Butterworth Trench. The latter attack just failed, but the bombing party succeeded in gaining some 100 yards and in blocking the trench not far from their objective after "an exceedingly bloody and brilliant attack." Later in the day (August 5th) the enemy made a small counter-attack against the new Durham positions, but this was easily repulsed. That same night the brigade was relieved, and (to quote the words of General Page Croft) "after 35 days' fighting or being shelled, during which we had only had five days' rest behind the guns, we marched on August 8th away from these bloody scenes and stayed at amazingly peaceful villages in the rear – in another world, where the eternal drab is replaced by the green of an innocent countryside."

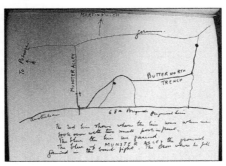

Map Showing Butterworth Trench

Citation:

Lieutenant George S.K. Butterworth. Near Pozieres from 17th to 19th July, 1916, commanded the Company, of which his Captain had been wounded, with great ability and coolness. By his energy and total disregard of personal safety he got his men to accomplish a good piece of work linking up the front line. I have already brought forward this officer's name for his work during the period 7th to 10th July, 1916.

MILITARY CROSS.

H. Wilkinson, Lieut.-Col. A.A., Q.M.G., 23rd Division.

Military Cross and Regimental Badges

MILITARY LETTERS

Letters from Captain Edward Borrow,
Adjutant, 13th Durham Light Infantry,

August 6th, 1916.
"The Commanding Officer, Capt. G. White, has asked me to write and inform you of the very serious loss we have suffered in the death of your son.

His talents as a Company Commander were undoubtedly great, and on the night of the 4/5th inst. when he was ordered to bomb up a trench and hold an important post, he personally supervised this work, so that now, as I write, the post, 20 yards from the enemy, remains in our hands.

Unfortunately it was this thoroughness in supervision which indirectly led to his death. The trench had been so knocked about by bombs and shells that some places were very exposed, and a German saw him soon after dawn on the 5th.

His brother officers and men dearly loved your son, and his absence from the Battalion will be greatly felt for a very long time to come."

August 8th.
"The Commanding Officer wishes me again to write to you and inform you that the Commander-in-Chief has awarded to your son the Military Cross.

This was awarded him for the very excellent work he did during July. He again earned the Cross on the night of his death, and the great regret of the Commanding Officer and all his fellow officers is that your son did not live long enough to know that his pluck and ability as a Company Commander had received some reward."

Letter from Capt. G. White,
Commanding 13th Battalion DLI,

August 10th, 1916.

"The G.O.C. 23rd Division instructs me to forward you the ribbon of the Military Medal which he would have personally presented to your son to-day had Lieut. Butterworth lived. I also enclose a short account of the circumstances for which this decoration has been awarded."

Letter from Brigadier-General H. Page Croft, C.M.G., M.P.,
Commanding 68th Infantry Brigade.

August 13th, 1916.

"I feel I must write you a small note to tell you how deeply I grieve with you and yours for the loss of your gallant son. He was one of those quiet, unassuming men whose path did not appear naturally to be a military one, and I have watched him doing his duty quietly and conscientiously. When the offensive came he seemed to throw off his reserve, and in those strenuous 35 days in which we were fighting off and on, he developed a power of leadership which we had not realised that he possessed. As you know, I recommended him for an earlier action near Contalmaison for the Military Cross, which alas! he could not wear. When in front of Pozieres he was reported to me to have done excellent work under very heavy fire in getting his men to dig a new trench right in front of the Germans, from which, later, the Australians were able to successfully attack that village. Later we went into a line on the right of the Australians, S.E. of Pozieres.

Here we were about 450 yards from the Germans, and I gave orders to dig a trench within 200 yards of them so that we could attack with some chance of success.

This trench was dug in a fog, and was a very fine deep trench which saved many lives in the days to follow, and your son again superintended the work, and it was called Butterworth Trench on all the official maps.

Three days afterwards the 13th D.L.I. attacked Munster Alley just N.W. of Butterworth Trench. They won 100 yards after a very hot fight, and I went up there at 4am in the morning to find the bomb fight still progressing, but the 13th holding their own. Your son was in charge, and the trench was very much blown in and shallow, and I begged him to keep his head down. He was cheery and inspiring his tired men to secure the position which had been won earlier in the night, and I felt that all was well with him there. The Germans had been bombing our wounded, and the men all round him were shooting Germans who showed themselves. Within about a minute of my leaving him he was shot, as I heard by telephone on my return. I could ill afford to lose so fine a soldier, and my deepest sympathy goes out to his relations, for I know that the loss of one so modest and yet so brave must create a gap which can never be filled."

Letter from Lieut.-Col. G.H. Ovens,
General of the 68th Brigade when in training.

27th August, 1916.

"I am so glad to have known your son and he was instrumental in bringing a fine lot of most valuable officers to the 68th Brigade. I did not know he was so very distinguished in music, but I realised that he was a valuable and capable officer, with much zeal and attention to detail and a very high zone. I am so glad that he had the opportunity of proving his worth before 'passing on.' I am sure he will be much regretted in the Brigade, which has, I believe, done very good service....Your son showed his grit by enlisting and wishing to remain longer in the ranks."

Letter from Lieut.-Col. R.O. Turner,
13th Durham Light Infantry.

19th August, 1916.

"I have, during the months of June and July been commanding the 13th D.L.I. (I am now home on sick leave), and saw a lot of your son's work. He was splendid – absolutely calm and collected, however unpleasant things were, and a magnificent example to his men, whom, incidentally, he looked after very well. I recommended him for the Military Cross, but as it is not awarded posthumously, I fear his death may have preceded the award."

APPRECIATIONS

"George Butterworth and his works." By H.P.A.

Reprinted from the Times Literary Supplement,
Thursday, April 26th, 1917.

'When George Butterworth was killed in action on August 5th, 1916, English music was robbed of one its most promising composers and national musical art of a stimulating force. His friends, who perhaps were unprepared for the high military gifts which he displayed in those last strenuous months of his life, were in no way surprised at the splendid manner of his death, for they had always recognised in him a fearless disregard for the consequences of action which he thought right, a Northern bluntness of speech which his men of the Durham Light Infantry were swift to appreciate and to respond to, and a thoroughness in detail and coolness of judgement which called forth the highest praise from his commanding officers.

A week or so before he was killed he had been slightly wounded near Pozieres. He was mentioned for distinguished work done July 7th-10th, and was awarded the Military Cross, although he did not live long enough to know this. On the night of his death he again earned it. In the map of that part of the line where Butterworth was in action at that time, a trench, which had been captured under his command and was held by him and his men, is officially marked as "Butterworth Trench".

But George Butterworth, with all these fine soldier qualities, was at heart a musician, and from his earliest years music had great attractions for him…

... Butterworth was thirty-one when he died. The number of compositions he left behind is not large; but before he went to France he set his papers in order and destroyed a large number of pieces (especially pianoforte works and songs) which to his mind did not seem sufficiently good to be preserved. The compositions which he left are, however, a fine achievement and, if he had not given his life to the greater cause, would have been the pledge of a great future. They are sincere, original, and beautiful. Although he was self-reliant, Butterworth was modest about the things he did best. Impatient of delay and intolerant of stupidity, he was extraordinarily careful of detail, and revised his work over and over again. He was one who 'searched out his spirit,' and who found it well-nigh impossible to satisfy himself.

The same qualities which distinguished him as a soldier would undoubtedly have brought him deserved renown as a composer. Courage, patience, initiative, wide sympathies, high motives, and the instinct of genius for the essential were all his; and those who knew him well had looked with no mistaken confidence to the day when he would hold a high place among British composers and would play a leading part in the fulfilment of the ideals which he cherished for the future of our national music.'

By R.V.W.

One of my grateful memories of George is connected with my "London Symphony," indeed I owe its whole idea to him. I remember very well how the idea originated. He had been sitting with us one evening talking, smoking and playing (I like to think that it was one of those rare occasions when we persuaded him to play us his beautiful little pianoforte piece, "Firle Beacon"), and at the end of the evening, just as he was getting up to go, he said, in his characteristically abrupt way, "You know, you ought to write a symphony." From that moment the idea of a symphony – a thing which I had always declared I would never attempt – dominated my mind. I shewed the sketches to George, bit by bit as they were finished, and it was then that I realised that he possessed, in common with very few composers, a wonderful power of criticism of other men's work and insight into their ideas and motives. I can never feel too grateful to him for all he did for me over this work and his help did not stop short at criticism. When Ellis suggested that my symphony should be produced at one of his concerts I was away from home and unable to revise the score myself, and George, together with Ellis and Francis Toye, undertook to revise it and to make a "short score" from the original – George himself undertook the last movement. There was a passage which troubled him very much, but I could never get him to say exactly what was wrong with it; all he would say was, "It won't do at all." After the performance he at once wrote to tell me he had changed his mind. He wrote:-

"A work cannot be a fine one until it is finely played, and it is still possible that _____ may turn out equally well. I really advise you not to alter a note of the symphony until after its second performance. The passages I kicked at didn't bother me at all, because the music as a whole is so definite that a little occasional meandering is pleasant rather than otherwise. As to the scoring, I frankly don't understand how it all comes of so well, but it does all sound right, so there's nothing more to be said."

Another musical meeting ground for George and myself was the English Folk-Song, for which he did so much and which did so much for him. It has often been my privilege to hear him improvise harmonies to the folk-tunes which he had collected, bringing out in them a beauty and character which I had not realised when simply looking at them. This was not merely a case of "clever harmonisation"; it meant that the inspiration which led to the original inception of these melodies and that which lay at the root of George's art were one and the same, and that in harmonising folk-tunes, or using them in his compositions, he was simply carrying out a process of revolution of which these primitive melodies and his own art are different stages.

When I first knew George's composition, the traces of that individuality, which was so pronounced later on, were indeed to be found, but hindered and checked, partly by the influence of Schumann and Brahms, and partly by what may be described as the "Oxford manner" in music – that fear of self-expression which seems to be fostered by academic traditions.

It was the folk-song which freed George's art from its foreign surroundings; to him the folk-song was a means of freedom, which enabled him to throw off the fetters that hindered his earlier efforts and formed a nucleus that focused his hitherto vague strivings after those things at which he really aimed. It is certain that his study of folk-song coincided with the development of his real musical self. With him the folk-song, as a basis of musical inspiration, was not merely "playing with local colour"; his most beautiful compositions, the "Shropshire Lad," for example, or the Henley songs, have no direct connection with any folk-tune, but their influence is no less clearly to be seen than in the "Idylls," in which he definitely took folk-music as the thematic basis. Indeed, he could no more help composing in his own national idiom than he could help speaking his own mother tongue.

The following article was written by George for the Magazine of the Royal College of Music after the first performance of the Symphony. His intimate association with the work at its inception gives the article a special interest apart from the quality of the writing. - A.K.B.

VAUGHAN WILLIAMS'S "LONDON" SYMPHONY"

"At length they all to merry London came,
To merry London, my most kindly nurse." – Spenser.

Mr. F.B. Ellis, whose recent series of concerts is noticed elsewhere, may be considered fortunate in having secured the first performances of at least one work of outstanding importance. The compositions of Vaughan Williams merit the attention of every serious student, not merely on account of their intrinsic musical value, but also as affording an unusually interesting example of the growth of a contemporary style. It would be hard to name any other first-rate composer who has 'found himself' with such apparent difficulty as Vaughan Williams, and this fact is sometimes cited against him as a proof of amateurish clumsiness; the beauty and originality of his ideas is widely recognised, but the not infrequent failure to express them clearly is usually ascribed to some inherent incapacity for perfecting a technique.

It would probably be more logical to blame the actual newness of the ideas themselves, and the necessity thus created for laborious working out of a new method. The same paradox applies in some measure to all composers of progressive tendency, but in the case of Vaughan Williams the labours of the preceding generation seem to have been of unusually little assistance; the absence of a characteristically native idiom may largely account for this, but it would be premature to attempt a final explanation. What is of more immediate importance is to recognise that in his later works Vaughan Williams has given evidence of having finally overcome what Mr. Edwin Evans aptly terms his 'impediment of musical speech'; hence the announcement of a full-bloodied symphony from his pen was calculated to raise hopes of something exceptionally good.

It may be said at once that these hopes have been fully realized; in this new work, almost for the first time the composer's ideas and their actual expression are really commensurate, and the success of the symphony was greatly enhanced by the magnificent performance given by the Queen's Hall Orchestra, under the direction of Mr. Geoffrey Toye – perhaps as good a 'first performance' as it would be possible to obtain.

As its title implies, the symphony is descriptive of London, more especially the London of to-day. It would be useless, without the aid of musical illustrations, to give an exhaustive analysis, and a short account of each movement must suffice.

A slow, mystical prelude – to be considered as introductory to the work as a whole – leads directly into the first movement proper, an exhilarating and expansive piece of music, which seems to owe its genesis to the stirring bustle of everyday life, and the busy turmoil of the London streets. The melodic material is very abundant, and many of the tunes have a distinctly 'popular' flavour about them; there is, of course, contrasting sections of more restrained character, but the general mood is boisterous, and the close a perfect orgy of triumph. This movement is certainly the most brilliant piece of orchestral writing that Vaughan Williams has as yet produced.

The slow movement is an idyll of grey skies and secluded by-ways – an aspect of London quite as familiar as any other; the feeling of the music is remote and mystical and its very characteristic beauty is not of a kind which it is possible to describe in words.

To the Scherzo is given the alternative title "Nocturne"; the combination is unexpected, but justified by the nature of the subject; after all to the average Londoner, the night is generally the time in which he is free to 'play.' It is not, however, a scene of conversational metropolitan gaiety which is depicted, but rather the careless freedom with which common folk disport themselves at night in the open streets. In addition to the "Scherzo" proper there are two "Trios," of which the second is in strong contrast with the rest of the movement.

The Finale is the longest of the four movements; perhaps also, it is the least satisfactory; not that there is any falling off in the interest, but, as in the last movement of the "Sea" Symphony, there is a feeling that the composer is straining himself to express just a little too much; in this case, however, the flaw is a much slighter one, and may easily prove to be illusory when the work is heard a second time. The music is for the most part strenuous, but in a different sense from that in which the first movement is so. It is the unrest of a conscious struggle which is here suggested.

When this mood has worked itself out, there is a return to the theme of the Prelude, which is treated at some length, and forms an impressive epilogue to the whole work.

It is now almost a common-place to say of a novelty that it was 'enthusiastically received'; the description means little or nothing, and yet there are occasions in which it is instinctively and generally felt that something out of the ordinary has been achieved. There can be no question as to the appeal which this work made to those who were present on March 27, and it is presumable that it would be equally successful with any normal English audience. The only question is whether it will be given the opportunity of becoming popular. The mere necessity for asking such a question shows up once again the astonishing conditions which govern the policy of concert-giving organisations in this country, and it is actually true that no arrangements have as yet been made for a second performance.

George Butterworth.

By R.L.

It is ten years since I first met George Butterworth. It was at a village concert at Heyford, to which he came from Oxford with Mr. Ferdinand Speyer, then music scholar of Balliol, to play sonatas of Beethoven, Mozart and Brahms. After that I saw him from time to time during that period of experiment, when he was, as it were, seeking for his real sphere of work – now giving himself seriously to piano playing, now writing musical criticism, and now teaching music at Radley.

But it was during the years immediately preceding the war that we saw the most of each other and became great friends. Composition and the collection of Morris Dances had become his settled purposes and kept him hard at work without making him "busy" in the fretful, urban way, which was always distasteful to him. I accompanied him several times on expeditions in search of Morris Dances. It was a fascinating quest, and his skill in discovering the real thing was amazing. He had a genius for avoiding a false scent.

I well remember the first time I met him at Bucknell, near Bicester, which was an important "hunting ground." I found him already at work in a picturesque and ancient cottage with a stone floor and white-washed walls and wheelbacked chair. An incredibly old man was dancing about the floor, and though sometimes he hobbled and stumbled or paused for sheer lack of breath, he seemed on the whole to have vanquished his years for a space and one felt a ghostly presence of revels that had had their being half-a-century before. George Butterworth sat by the wall, smoking his pipe, mostly in silence, and busily noting the dancer's steps in a book. Now and then he would put a question or suddenly demand the repetition of a particular figure. But the dancer paid little attention to us and passed from one dance to another as the fragrance of youthful memories inspired him. And George let him have his way, for he knew that he had found a first-class exponent of the art. Later we called on the old man's brother, who also danced for us regardless of exhaustion and the obvious anxiety of his middle-aged daughter.

But the most amazing performance occurred a few days later. A piper, who used sometimes to pipe for the dancers in old days, had been fetched from a neighbouring village and the two old brothers had come out into the street to dance. They were already at it when I arrived. It was a summer evening; George Butterworth was standing in the middle of the village street, pencil and notebook in hand. He was intent only upon the dancing and entirely oblivious of the crowd of bewildered villagers, who had collected to see the unwanted spectacle. On the road beside him was a heap of notebooks; on the other side, also in the road, an immense jug of beer, the reservoir from which the dancers drew fresh stores of energy. A little way off, a piper, a man of some fifty or sixty years, was blowing his pipe and beating the little "tabor" or drum which hung round his neck, and producing by these means a most naïve and alluring frolic of sound. In the midst the aged dancers were dancing as they had not danced for a generation or more. They carried handkerchiefs which they waved and made great play of, according to the elaborate ritual of the Morris. They advanced and retired, they bowed and they capered, they executed intricate figures with the comrades, who were present to their minds, though in fact they had lain many years in the neighbouring churchyard. The old men were obviously elated at finding one who could admire and appreciate their art as it had been admired and appreciated when they were young. They were proudly scornful of the ignorant and astonished crowd of villagers. It was a strange scene and amusing in many ways, but the crowd was too much astonished to laugh, and they was something about it all that was strangely enthralling, for every now and then, even in this curiously mutilated exhibition, one caught glimpses of an art-form which, for all its rusticity and naiveté, had a mysterious beauty like some of Shakespeare's songs.

There is no doubt that Morris Dancing meant a great deal to George Butterworth at this time, and this was the period of his greatest creative activity as a composer. Whatever may be thought of the theory which he held, that music ought to be national and that German music, for example, is essentially an alien thing to the English musician, there can be no doubt that in English folk-music he found a source of inspiration peculiarly suited to his genius. He was not of the order of modern artists who find completeness of expression in a language of complex texture, elaborately qualified and overlaid with multitudinous shades of meaning. At the same time his art did not express itself by means of inspired impromptus. He worked and almost painfully, and if the alphabet of his artistic speech had been anything less simple and direct than folk-music, it is difficult to see how he could ever have attained to that special style which is so entirely himself.

When his music came to be understood and was highly valued, it was remarkable how inclined he was to despise the pleasure which appreciation naturally gave him. At Leeds it was difficult to persuade him that the applause required his presence on the platform, and at Oxford, when one of his orchestral pieces was received with enthusiastic delight, I remember that amid all the clapping of hands his predominant feeling was one of indignation with a harpist who had, he asserted, played her part precisely as he had told her not to play it.

George Butterworth hated shams of all kinds and humbled every impudent insincerity that he met. But for anything genuine, warm-hearted and courageous he had more than admiration, whether he found it on a village cricket field, or in a rustic public house, or in the mud of Flanders. When he came home from France on leave, I had lunch with him one day and his talk was chiefly about the Durham miners of his regiment. In them he found the salt of the earth. They would certainly beat the Germans he said, for no German had their strength or endurance. There was nothing like their intelligence to the outrageous assaults of evil weather; through hours of incessant rain they would deliberately scorn the protection of a great coat. Besides, they knew a lot of good folk-tunes; he had learnt several new ones from his men. George Butterworth had in fact a genius for sincerity, alike in art and in life. Sincerity is a goal which many modernist artists strive to attain, but often the effort is conscious and painful, and they achieve nothing better than calculated sincerity. With George Butterworth sincerity was the starting point not the goal. Everything that he did, everything that he said, every note of his music, was sincere and true. I shall remember him as one of the strongest and truest men I have ever known.

I think the following passages from appreciative letters written to me soon after George's death, mostly by musicians whose own work is well known and some of whom were personally unknown, or only slightly known, to George or me, may be interesting to George's friends, as they were to me, as adding emphasis to the views elsewhere expressed on the quality of his musical gifts. A.K.B.

"We all felt how full of promise life was for him and what fine things would come from him, of which the beautiful and manly work that he had already given us was only a fore-taste. As I write I can see him now, as we first met, when one morning quite early he called here, with his arms full of some hundreds of songs that he had collected....He was so eager and so absolutely sincere and so wonderfully gifted. His splendid song-cycle, with its moving prophetic words is a wonderful monument. There was a fine rugged beauty in all his work, which was the promise of the really great musician." L.E.B

"Art too has lost much. He wrote with so much sanity, sincerity and purpose." A.E.B.

"The Editor of 'The Times' has passed on your letter to me. I had intended before receiving it to write to you to add my word to the many you must have received telling you how others valued your son and feel his loss. I knew him well. ...I remember especially a morning we spent together in the picture gallery at Leeds during the last festival when his orchestral piece 'The Cherry Tree' was played, and we met again for the last time at the rehearsals of Vaughan Williams' 'London Symphony' in the spring before the war. I got him then to write a little about the symphony for the R.C.M. Magazine, which I then edited, and his keen delight in the work was what struck me most. That all seems long ago, and I have often thought hopefully of what he, and the others who like him went straight off to join the colours when war was declared, would be able to do for music when all the horror was over. ... At any rate he has left good things behind him. It was only the other day that another composer was speaking to me of his songs as among the most beautiful in the English Language." H.C.C.

"Permit me, a total stranger, to offer a tribute of sympathy and esteem to you in the loss of your son. I, a musician, in some degree...feel that his death is a national loss, comparable to that of Rupert Brooke. Perhaps in a slight measure the knowledge that the composer of 'Is My Team Ploughing?' does not pass unrecognised as regards his truly real achievement may be of consolation to you and his family." C.E.C.

"I can hardly expect you to remember me, for it is nearly thirty years since you once spent a Sunday at R____, but the recollection of Mrs. Butterworth's beautiful singing – she sang *'Saper vorreste'* from *'Un Ballo in Maschera'* – is one of the most vivid impressions of my childhood. She talked about George then; but I never met him until after he had left Eton, and had already written music of note. I used to see him occasionally at Oxford and in London, but never had the chance of becoming intimate with him. People write so much now about the military achievements of those who have been killed that there is a danger of their real normal work being overlooked: and I feel that this is important in George's case because he left so little written. But that little was enough to show – so I thought – that he would have accomplished very great things. The rhapsody was a most beautiful piece of work: perfectly finished in technique, so clearly designed, so certain and so masterly in its execution: and so full of wonderful beauty and poetry – not a note in it that was not deeply significant. That certainly was his own personal character: he was absolutely incapable of producing clichés, half-felt stuff. And I felt the more certain of my judgement because I did not know him intimately, and had none of that predisposition to understand, which naturally helps one with a new work by a composer who is one's intimate friend. Indeed, I felt that it was his music which helped me to understand the nature which he had such a difficulty in expressing in ordinary ways. His death is the greatest loss that our modern music has suffered, a loss not only to his friends, but to all lovers of music, present and future." E.J.D.

"The copy of the score of the 'Rhapsody' recalls that day at the Leeds Festival when it was first performed and we all congratulated ourselves on the new voice that had come into English music. He will rank, with Brooke and Julian Grenfell, among the real poets who, in this war, have given their lives for their country. The loss, not only to us who were his friends, but to all who came within his influence, must needs seem irreparable.

Yet the Music will live – 'Great in what it achieved, greater still in what it promised' – and will remind future generations that England gave her best to the sacrifice. ...You will always have the memory of what he was and of the love and admiration in which he was held by all who knew him." W.H.H.

"I heard 'A Shropshire Lad' at Leeds Festival, and recognised then its remarkable qualities and first-rate workmanship. ...I am glad of the opportunity of adding my little testimony to the great musical gifts which your son undoubtedly possessed. I knew him pretty well: for I saw him frequently in Oxford and London in the pre-war days. English music is undeniably the poorer for his loss, and many of us will be glad that we have in print at any rate one piece of evidence of the great promise which was not permitted to come to complete fulfilment." C.B.R.

"I should like, if you would allow me, to express my very deep sympathy with you in the loss of your son, whom I had known for a long time. I had a cordial admiration for his compositions, and the firmest belief in his musical future." E.W.

... "It is terrible to think of the sudden close of a career that promised to be a peculiarly brilliant one. He was greatly respected and beloved by all our [Folk] dancing people in England, and there must be many, like myself, now mourning his loss." C.J.S.

"I have been asked by the Committee and members of the English Folk Dance Society to write and express our very deep sympathy with you in your loss. You will understand how much your son will be missed by all of us who knew him so well and have worked with him for so long. We feel that not only have we lost a great personal friend, but one of the leading spirits of our Society, whose place can never be filled." H.K.

"The Society has sustained irreparable loss in the death of Mr. R.J.E. Tiddy, Mr. Perceval Lucas, Mr. G.J. Wilkinson and Mr. George Butterworth, who gave up their lives for their country at the Battle of the Somme. They had all been keen and active supporters of the Society from its foundation in December, 1911, and given to it, unselfishly and ungrudgingly, of their best. . . . . . Mr. George Butterworth joined the committee in its early days and remained a member of it to the last. He was a strong and spirited dancer and held a prominent position in the original men's Morris side. He was a brilliant musician, who, had he lived, would assuredly have followed up the success which the performance of his Rhapsody achieved at the Leeds Musical Festival in 1913. He was a fine pianist – who will forget his playing of 'Bonny Green'? – a collector both of folk songs and dances, author of *Folk Songs from Sussex* and co-editor of the third and fourth Country Dance Books and fifth Morris Book." (from *The English Folk Dance Society Report*, 1916)

"I am sure you will be pleased to hear that your son's Rhapsody for orchestra was a great success at the Promenade Concert [6/9/17]. I have put the Rhapsody down for one of the Sunday Afternoon Concerts at the Queen's Hall. ...The work made a great impression upon all who heard it; there is such a beautiful atmosphere about it, and the scoring is masterly." H.J.W.

[This letter was written by Sir Henry Wood after the performance of the Rhapsody at the Queen's Hall on September 6th, 1917. – A.K.B.]

POSTSCRIPT

By "D."

I have been asked to write a postscript to this little volume of George Butterworth for two reasons; first, but not foremost, because circumstances brought us much together during his last few years and broke down outer shells of reserve; and secondly, because I have before me many appreciative letters from friends, to whom also he clearly meant much, and so perhaps can select from these letters and from my own knowledge some further light on sides of his strong personality not much over dwelt on in the admirable memoirs of Dr. Allen and Mr. Morris.

The letter that comes first to my mind is one from a friend who saw much of him in music and holiday mood from his early Oxford days. Many letters touch the same note, but this perhaps appeals to me as the most completely expressed. It says – "Amongst the Oxford men whom I have come to know in music George stands out as the most original, the most impatient of humbug, the most gifted in the real meaning of things, and the most (to me) attractive personality, for he combined great shyness with great power, and roughness with a very tender heart and was altogether lovable."

Another Oxford friend writes of him, "I never met a man who spoke so little and with such extraordinarily independent and sane judgement when he did." A true note also, and one that recalls meetings when he was very silent and many others when he talked much on a variety of topics, and always with something interesting to say. He did not readily impart from a habit of being silent unless he had something he really wished to say, though I remember his doing so on at least one occasion to help a friend with a dull dinner party. That seems to make it natural to pick out next a letter from the mother of a school and University friend at whose house George was a frequent and always welcome guest from early school days. She says "he was always the quiet thoughtful one of the boys who helped everyone." Another old friend writes "he was such a splendid fellow and such a kind good friend," and later, "what he enlisted to fight for I know he felt was worth dying for." There are many letters one would like to quote, because not everyone got below his sometimes rough and impatient outside shell, but most of them emphasize the same strong features, notable even in boyish days. An early tutor at home remembers him as "a boy of honour and gentleness, incapable of anything unworthy." A schoolfellow says that "he never seemed to think of himself at all, and I expect that was why we were all so fond of him in College"; and another that "he possessed mental and moral courage to a far higher degree than anyone else I ever knew. He was utterly incapable of any mean or ungenerous thought," and yet another that "he had a fine, clear, uncompromising brain; everyone who knew him at all was impressed by his personality as by something big." The father of a college friend writes "I got to like George so much and I felt he was such a fine sterling character, full of noble qualities and great mainlines and pluck. My son used to tell me what a splendid character he was, and such a true, honest and brave disposition."

There are many more one might add, but they repeat the same theme and this after all is a postscript. Those referring specially to his music, and others from masters and tutors, will have been read elsewhere in this little volume.

Besides his general lovableness, I think the most strong impression George made on me was the splendid balance of his character and brain, and his fine sense of proportion. He had, to a marked degree, Rhodes' ideal qualities of "manhood, truth, courage, devotion to duty, sympathy for and protection of the weak, kindliness, unselfishness and fellowship." And with these qualities an intolerance of insincerity, of stupidity of all kinds, of mental and moral weakness combined with a large measure of tender consideration for real physical weakness and suffering, although himself of too fine physique to have experienced much of either. Confident in debate, emphatic in opinion, he was yet modest in all his attainments – his modesty about his music one of his old friends describes as amounting to "almost a disease" – and this same modesty has lost to us some compositions that are much regretted by those who have heard them, for before he went on active service he destroyed all manuscripts that did not touch the high mark he set for himself. With his modesty and shy retirement he was yet so unconventional in many ways that people were often deceived at first by the rougher surface he showed them.

One could rely on his being wise, just, and careful, as well as generous in expending himself, on anything he considered of real importance to those he cared for, though quite often he would not render them purely conventional 'service.' Vivid memories crowd in of the amount of cheery energy and care he put into wheeling an invalid chair through Hampstead lanes; into packing the belongings – not a job he liked! – of a sick friend, and manoeuvring a station Bath chair along a crowded platform; also of his omission, probably accompanied with a growl, to perform some of the small customary courtesies. Memories too of the infinite pains he took for the well-being of those he cared for in their more solid and lasting difficulties or problems. But if one tried to thank him, he would be truly embarrassed and retreat with some of his favourite ejaculations, "absurd, impossible, ridiculous, hopeless," or begin talking hard on another subject.

When war broke out he realised, more than most, some of the immediate results. He was folk-dancing at Stratford at that time and I was in Germany for a "cure." He realised at once that my position there would be very difficult and unpleasant, and, too, that a man of military age would run a grave risk by entering Germany then; yet he at once telegraphed to his father offering to try to reach me and help me home. He was indeed a good friend; and a good citizen also. It was not only in his military service that he recognised the responsibilities of nationality. He had a carefully acquired and sound knowledge of contemporary politics, and took a keen interest in labour, social, and other national problems. His grasp was both comprehensive and quick. He was thorough in this as in all else and often original in his conclusions. He might be – often was – slow to act or take responsibility, but whatever he did undertake, he carried out thoroughly – small things and large ones, all well done and completed. Few men could be less suited by inclination and tastes for a soldier's life; yet he had no hesitation at all, but joined the lowest rank and worked hard and whole-heartedly to make himself the fine soldier and leader of men he proved in those last months. As the Head of his College wrote, "we could see he disliked it all more than most, but he was as keen as possible." One of the letters before me recalls meeting some men of his regiment at Hindhead shortly before they left for France, and that they said "the men all love Lieutenant Butterworth and would do anything for him." It is good to know, as we do from several sources, that he was appreciated by the ruggedly strong North Company miners he commanded: another instance of his "sane judgement," for he carefully considered, both as a private and as an officer, what regiment he should join – rejecting with emphatic impatience someone's suggestion that it should be one of the so-called "gentleman's battalions" – and he had a great, almost affectionate, admiration for the men under him in France, expressed with much enthusiastic warmth on his last leave home, early in June. He was in splendid form that leave: wonderful when one considers his sensitive nature and what he had just been through and expected to go through. One of his friends he cared much for writes of this leave "We had the happiest meeting with him on his last leave here. It was such a pleasure to see him so strong and confident, and I felt then what a power and comfort he must be to his men."

One can picture him at the dawn of the 5th of August, smoking his pipe, well content with his success in capturing the trench. That job was done, and well done, and he had the good workman's satisfaction in an aim achieved – as surely often before in happier fields – while full of pride for "those splendid fellows," the Durham miners, whom he was cheering and encouraging to the very end.

George

So thou hast died for England! with thy boys
Around thee. Sad and strange it seems to me
That thou should'st die this death, when peaceful joys,
Creative art, music and song, (for thee
Thy rightful heritage, and proper aim)
Were thine. Thy country called thee! Age to man,
And beast, a faithful friend, to kill and main
Was alien to thy kindly nature's plan.
'Whom the gods love, die young.' It must have been
Inferno to thy gentle soul! Hell's noise,
Such frightful sounds, and sights, the world's ne'er seen!
But, borne aloft on Death's soft, sable wing,
Thou hearest, now, the Heavenly Voices sing.

'In Memorium G.S.K.B.', by 'M.E.B.', 13 August 1916

A LAST POST...

*"I sometimes dread coming back to normal life with so many gaps –
especially, of course, George Butterworth...." R.V.W.*

IN MEMORY OF...
CAPTAIN **HUGH MONTAGU BUTTERWORTH**
9TH BATTALION RIFLE BRIGADE
WHO DIED AGE 29 ON 25TH SEPTEMBER, 1915
SON OF GEORGE MONTAGU BUTTERWORTH AND
CATHERINE LUCIE BUTTERWORTH (NEE WARDE)
OF THE CASHMEER HILLS, CHRISTCHURCH, NEW ZEALAND.
MASTER AT WANGANUI COLLEGIATE SCHOOL, NEW ZEALAND
REMEMBERED WITH HONOUR
MENIN GATE MEMORIAL

IN MEMORY OF...
LIEUTENANT **PHILIP ANTHONY BROWN**
13TH BATTALION DURHAM LIGHT INFANTRY
WHO DIED AGE 29 ON 4TH NOVEMBER, 1915
REMEMBERED WITH HONOUR
RATION FARM MILTARY CEMETERY

IN MEMORY OF...
SERGEANT **GEORGE JERRARD WILKINSON**
16TH BATTALION MIDDLESEX REGIMENT
WHO DIED AGE 29 ON 1ST JULY, 1916
MUSICIAN AND COMPOSER.
REMEMBERED WITH HONOUR
THIEPVAL MEMORIAL

IN MEMORY OF...
SECOND LIEUTENANT **PERCIVAL DREWETT LUCAS**
2ND BATTALION BORDER REGIMENT
WHO DIED AGE 36 ON 6TH JULY, 1916
REMEMBERED WITH HONOUR
ABBEVILLE COMMUNAL CEMETERY

IN MEMORY OF...
CAPTAIN **ROBERT COMBER WOODHEAD**
12TH BATTALION DURHAM LIGHT INFANTRY
WHO DIED ON 17TH JULY, 1916
REMEMBERED WITH HONOUR
THIEPVAL MEMORIAL

IN MEMORY OF...
LIEUTENANT **GEORGE SAINTON KAYE BUTTERWORTH** M.C.
13TH BATTALION DURHAM LIGHT INFANTRY
WHO DIED AGE 31 ON 5TH AUGUST, 1916
SON OF SIR ALEXANDER KAYE BUTTERWORTH, KT., LL.B.,
OF 16 FROGNAL GARDENS, HAMPSTEAD, LONDON, AND
THE LATE JULIA MARGUERITE (NEE WIGAN) HIS WIFE.
REMEMBERED WITH HONOUR
THIEPVAL MEMORIAL

IN MEMORY OF...
LIEUTENANT **REGINALD JOHN ELLIOTT TIDDY**
2ND/4TH BATTALION
OXFORD AND BUCKS LIGHT INFANTRY
WHO DIED AGE 36 ON 10TH AUGUST, 1916
REMEMBERED WITH HONOUR
LAVENTIE MILITARY CEMETERY, LA GORGUE

IN MEMORY OF...
COMPANY SERGEANT MAJOR
FREDRICK HILLDERSON KEELING
16TH BATTALION DUKE OF CORNWALL'S LIGHT INFANTRY
WHO DIED ON 18TH AUGUST, 1916
REMEMBERED WITH HONOUR
THIEPVAL MEMORIAL

IN MEMORY OF...
CAPTAIN **FRANCIS BEVIS ELLIS**
10TH BN., NORTHUMBERLAND FUSILIERS
WHO DIED ON 26TH SEPTEMBER, 1916
A MUSICIAN.
REMEMBERED WITH HONOUR
ADANAC MILITARY CEMETERY, MIRAUMONT

IN MEMORY OF...
LIEUTENANT COMMANDER
FREDERICK SEPTIMUS KELLY D.S.C.
ROYAL NAVY VOLUNTEER RESERVE "HOOD"
WHO DIED AGE 35 ON 13TH NOVEMBER, 1916
REMEMBERED WITH HONOUR
MARTINSART BRITISH CEMETERY

IN MEMORY OF...
SECOND LIEUTENANT
AUBREY BARRINGTON-KENNETT
2ND BATTALION OXFORD AND BUCKS LIGHT INFANTRY
WHO DIED AGE 24 ON 20TH SEPTEMBER, 1914
REMEMBERED WITH HONOUR
VAILLY BRITISH CEMETERY

IN MEMORY OF...
MAJOR **BASIL HERBERT BARRINGTON-KENNETT**
2ND BATTALION GRENADIER GUARDS
WHO DIED AGE 30 ON 18TH MAY, 1915.
REMEMBERED WITH HONOUR
LE TOURET MILITARY CEMETERY, RICHEBOURG-L'AVOUE

IN MEMORY OF...
MAJOR **VICTOR ANNESLEY BARRINGTON-KENNETT**
4TH SQUADRON ROYAL FLYING CORPS
FORMERLY, GRENADIER GUARDS
WHO DIED ON 13TH MARCH, 1916
REMEMBERED WITH HONOUR
MIRAUMONT COMMUNAL CEMETERY

IN MEMORY OF........

From Five Photographs:
Two Taken in Childhood,
One at Eton (Speech Day),
One at Leeds (1913), and
One Folk Dancing at Stratford-on-Avon

Opposite is a copy of a list prepared by George and printed in 1912 or 1913. The title of the Henley Songs cycle, "Love blows as the Wind blows," is taken from the head-piece to the second song. The first lines of the four songs are:- (1) "In the year that's come and gone." (2) "Life in her creaking shoes." (3) "Fill a glass with golden wine." (4) "On the way to Kew." The work described as "Prelude – The Cherry Trees," is identical with the Rhapsody, "A Shropshire Lad." He found difficulty in settling the title of this work and up to the last moment hesitated between "The Land of Lost Content" and the title which he finally decided upon. After the date of this list George composed the three idylls on folk-tunes for small orchestra, the orchestral arrangements of the Henley songs and the suite for strings.... These are the only works which he preserved when he went through his papers preparatory to leaving for France, but a friend has lately sent me two further songs, slight in character, and evidently early in date, entitled "Crown Winter with Green," and "Haste on my Joys."
– A.K.B.

LIST OF COMPOSITIONS, &C.,

BY GEORGE BUTTERWORTH

VOICE AND PIANOFORTE.

Cycle of Six Songs from "A Shropshire Lad." (A.E. Housman.)
Augener, Ltd., 63, Conduit Street, W. Net, 3/-
1. Loveliest of Trees.
2. When I was One-and-Twenty.
3. Look not in My Eyes.
4. Think no more, Lad.
5. The Lads in their Hundreds.
6. Is my Team Ploughing?

"Bredon Hill" and other Songs from "A Shropshire Lad."
Augener, Ltd. Net, 3/-
1. Bredon Hill.
2. O fair enough are Sky and Plain.
3. When the Lad for longing sighs.
4. On the Idle Hill of Summer.
5. With Rue my Heart is Laden.

Eleven Folk-Songs from Sussex, collected and arranged.
Augener, Ltd. Net, 2/6

Two Songs for Baritone (MS.)
1. I Fear Thy Kisses (Shelley).
2. Requiescat (Wilde).

S.A.T.B.

"On Christmas Night." Traditional Carol.

Augener, Ltd. Net, 3d.

T.T.B.B.

"We get up in the Morn." Traditional Harvest Song.

Augener, Ltd. Net, 3d.

THREE-PART FEMALE CHOIR AND PIANOFORTE.

"In the Highlands." (Stevenson).

Augener, Ltd. Net, 6d.

BARITONE AND STRING QUARTET.

"Love blows as the Wind blows." (Henley). Cycle of Four Songs with alternative accompaniment for Pianoforte. (MS.)

FULL ORCHESTRA.

Prelude. - "The Cherry Tree." (MS.)

NOTICES OF CONCERTS

Mr. McInnes' Song Recital,

June, 1911.

Excellent as is the singer's record, he has done nothing finer than the recital he gave last night in Aeolian Hall, and it is small wonder that so many encores were exacted.

A very interesting new set of six songs from 'A Shropshire Lad' by Mr. George Butterworth was introduced; the folk-song character of the third is most successfully treated, and in 'Think no more, lad,' the composer has caught the reckless mood of the words very happily. 'The lads in their hundred's' was sung with fine *mezza voce* at the beginning and was encored, but the last, the grim 'Is my team ploughing,' is the finest of all. Two melodies are used, and are identified with the living and the dead man respectively; all is kept on the simplest plane, and the pathetic suggestion of the last line is irresistible. – *The Times*

A group of new songs by Mr. George Butterworth, which were brought forward by Mr. Campbell McInnes in the course of his vocal recital at Aeolian Hall last night, contained more promise of future success than proof of present attainment. By choosing words from Mr. Housman's 'Shropshire Lad' the composer has invited damaging comparisons between his own work and that of more mature song-writers. His studied avoidance of mere melodic attractiveness did not constitute a source of distinction or strength, but rather showed that he had mistrusted his own instincts and substituted effort for inspiration. – *Morning Post.*

A new song-cycle, 'A Shropshire Lad,' by George Butterworth, which was introduced, was of musical and poetic interest. The composer has in most of the six songs very happily reflected the sentiment of A. E. Housman's distinctive verses in music, which in its archaic character and model type suggests the folk-song spirit. – *Standard.*

Mr. J. Campbell McInnes did much better and achieved more variety of colour in a new setting by Mr. George Butterworth of six lyrics from Mr. A. E. Housman's 'Shropshire Lad.' Many of the songs have simplicity of design that is appropriate and effective, though possibly a trifle too conscious in some cases. It is admirably used in 'The Lads in their Hundreds,' however, the graceful melody of which ensured its repetition. – *Daily News.*

Oxford Classical Concert,

February, 1912.

At the third of the present season of Public Classical Concerts at Oxford, given on Thursday night under Dr. H. P. Allen's direction, the programme included (along with Mozart's G Minor Symphony, Bach's Fifth Brandenburg Concerto and Brahms's 'Haydn Variations') two new English works for the first time of performance, both taking folk music as their basis…….Equally cordial was the reception of the other novelty, two 'Idylls in English Folk-tunes,' by Mr. George Butterworth, works not yet, perhaps, quite sure in touch, but of the highest promise, showing great individuality of harmony and orchestration and a singularly fresh and subtle imaginativeness. – *The Times.*

Leeds Musical Festival

October 2nd, 1913 – Newspaper Notices.

Mr. Butterworth's rhapsody, conducted by Herr Nikisch, preceded the motet, and Beethoven's Seventh Symphony followed it. Mr. Butterworth, like several of the younger English composers, has been a good deal attracted by the poems of A. E. Housman's 'A Shropshire Lad.' He has published two sets of songs from them, and the principal ideas of this rhapsody come from his setting of 'Loveliest of Trees.' Unless one knows the poem and his music to it one may miss the point of the rhapsody by not realizing what has set his imagination to work....

From the haunting call of four notes with which the rhapsody begins onward to the end there is a delicate fancy underlying all the music. It is slight, and the ideas only just bear the amount of development and extension given to them. A little more and all would have been lost, but as it is it makes a charming little piece full of suggestive colouring, though perhaps 'Fantasy' would have been a better title than 'Rhapsody.' It was excellently played and sympathetically received. The composer was called to the platform and came rather reluctantly. – *The Times.*

One hearing convinces that Mr. Butterworth's piece is the work of one having something to say, but it is more of a promise than an actual achievement. I liked his music best when it was simplest; then also it was freshest. The Rhapsody is based upon a song – also by Mr. Butterworth – a setting of 'The Cherry Tree,' from A. E. Housman's cycle, 'A Shropshire Lad.' It has a comparatively long introductory section, but after the statement of the subject matter the development is admirably managed, and the little work, which surely should be heard in London, made a very good impression indeed under Nikisch's guidance. – *Daily Telegraph.*

The morning programme was completed by orchestral numbers. One was a Rhapsody entitled 'A Shropshire Lad,' composed by Mr. George Butterworth, a Yorkshire musician clearly of considerable attainment. His Rhapsody is based on a song forming part of a cycle on A. E. Housman's poem of this name, and is therefore a disquisition on known matter. It is imaginative and resourceful, but chiefly remarkable for its promise of development in due course. It was conducted by Herr Nikisch, very finely played, and warmly acknowledged in the presence of the composer. – *Morning Post.*

..... Without going into superlatives it can be said without hesitation that in the Rhapsody Mr. Butterworth has shown himself to be an admirable student of his art, and he ought to go far in his profession. The prelude, which is quite descriptive, reflects a genuine musical temperament that has undergone a fitting training. There is much that is poetical in the work, but perhaps its best feature is its beautiful smoothness of rhythm. The climaxes are both well worked up, and the manner in which the diminuendo is made smoothly to succeed, displays real artistry in composition. Mr. Butterworth was accorded a fine reception at the close, having to bow his acknowledgement. He must have been delighted with the sympathetic reading given to the work by the orchestra, and with the fact that it was an effort that obviously pleased the conductor, Professor Nikisch. – *Yorkshire Herald.*

. . . . Goethe once wrote to a friend who understood the poetic side of his nature: 'When I was a boy I planted a cherry tree and watched its growth with delight.' . . . . Mr. Housman's 'A Shropshire Lad' also had a vision of a cherry tree, and Mr. Butterworth made a song of it. Having done this, he was minded to elaborate the theme of his song into the rhapsody we heard yesterday. It begins with a diaphanous introduction, in the modern French manner, and presently we have the song itself. In the working-out, one cadence-like phrase is eloquently insisted on by the strings in octaves, and another figure by the brass, but it is an unrealisable boy's dream after all, and the instruments sink back to their original vague and shimmering preludising. The rhapsody hits the mark as a home-sick musical reverie, and presents some charming instrumentation. The composer was wise enough to leave the conducting of his work to Herr Nikisch, but in response to continued applause he was induced to make his bow from the platform at the end. – *Yorkshire Observer.*

The second part of the concert began with one of the new works, the orchestral piece by Mr. George Butterworth which he entitles 'A Shropshire Lad' and describes as a Rhapsody. From the circumstance that it was originally named, in the early editions of the programme, 'The Cherry Tree,' and described as a 'Prelude,' one may surmise that the composer had some difficulty in settling upon a name for a composition which professes no poetic intention capable of definition by a title. The fact that the principle theme is taken from a song, 'The Cherry Tree,' which is one of a cycle entitled collectively 'The Shropshire Lad,' explains why these were hit upon in turn as titles, and to discover the initial motive that inspired the composer it is necessary to turn to the song. This is in effect the meditation of the 'Shropshire Lad' when exiled from his native land, a conception quite capable of musical expression, and one which must have been present to the composer when he evolved the melody. Beyond this the relationship of the Rhapsody to its title is not obvious, and it is safer to regard it as a simple effort to produce a well-balanced and pleasant-sounding piece of music, put together in musicianly style, but not revealing as yet, any marked individuality either in the thoughts or in the form in which they are expressed. Mr Butterworth is already a musician of considerable accomplishment, and his score shows no weak places, while his ideas, if not particularly new, are refined, and it may certainly be said that there is evidence of a genuinely poetic temperament in his music, which was very sympathetically played under the direction of Mr. Nikisch, who brought out its expressive qualities well. It was warmly received and the young composer . . . . had to yield to persistent applause, and show himself on the platform, Mr. Nikisch, to whom he had wisely entrusted the conductor's duty, meanwhile returning appealing looks and gestures, as much as to say 'It is not I, but another whom you must thank'. – *Yorkshire Post*.

Mr. F.B Ellis's Concert of
Modern Orchestral Music, Queen's Hall

March 20ᵗʰ, 1914 - Newspaper Notices.
The first of the interesting series of concerts which Mr. F.B. Ellis is giving to replace those of Mr. Balfour Gardiner was held at Queen's Hall last night and contained new works by Mr.

Arnold Bax and Mr. George Butterworth. The concert began with Mr. Arnold Bax's genial festival overture, which has been played several times, and this was followed by Mr. Butterworth's rhapsody, 'A Shropshire Lad,' first played at the Leeds Festival last year. With it came a new 'Idyll' by the same composer, called 'The Banks of Green Willow,' a piece written upon two folk-tunes, which carries on and develops the poetic feeling of the beautiful melodies very gracefully. – *The Times*.

Promenade Concert (Queen's Hall).

September 6th, 1917.

George Butterworth's Rhapsody made a welcome reappearance. It was performed first at Leeds, four years ago, and again in the spring of the next year at one of Mr. F.B. Ellis's concerts, Mr. Geoffrey Toye conducting. It was not well placed in the programme; its light touch and its economy of resources would have come better between the Berlioz and the Mozart. It is unconventional, because you cannot prophesy at any moment what is coming next, and scholarly, because you are sure that nothing will come that is irrelevant. This is obviously not the sort of music to like or dislike irrevocably at a single hearing, and one hopes that the orchestra will prosecute the acquaintance they have made with it, and give us another opportunity of realising what it is we have lost in the composer's early death and of remembering in what cause it was lost. – *The Times*.

Lieut. Butterworth's rhapsody is the epilogue to his musical setting of Housman's poem, 'A Shropshire Lad,' and was first heard at the

Leeds Festival of 1913. It was then described in these columns as showing 'imagination and resource.' Lieut. Butterworth's melodic idiom has the outstanding merit of being British. The harmonic investment shows a keenness of ear and feeling for colour expressed by means that are a testimony to his erudition. As indicated four years ago there is immense promise in the work; to-day one can but regret that there is no possibility of its fulfilment. – *Morning Post.*

Very decided character was given to the 'popular' programme of the Promenade Concert last night by the inclusion of a rhapsody, 'A Shropshire Lad,' by the late and much-lamented Lieut. George Butterworth, M.C., a composer of the greatest promise. His two cycles of settings of Housman's poems are fairly familiar, at least to the cognoscenti, but for some reason it has taken years for this orchestral work to reach London – or perhaps for no other than the ordinary reason. . . . It is a work of real distinction; its purpose is to give a kind of reminiscent impression of one of the songs, 'Loveliest of Trees, the cherry now is hung with bloom.' The haze and heat of a spring day, the fragrance of the bloom, the beauty of life on such a day, all seem in this music, a most worthy example of the great talent of a musical son of this land, now 'gone west' ere his prime. – *Daily Telegraph.*

The clever, picturesque rhapsody, 'A Shropshire Lad,' . . . . was originally produced at the last Leeds Festival and at once gave its composer . . . a place among the young composers of the day. The music, based upon ideas taken from Housman's poem of the same name, has a good deal of atmosphere, and its orchestration is effective. Well played by the Queen's Hall Orchestra, under Sir Henry Wood, it had a sympathetic reception. – *Daily Chronicle.*

The charming and picturesque orchestral rhapsody, 'A Shropshire Lad,' by the late Lieut. Butterworth, M.C., shows that a promising young musician was lost to this country by the untimely death of its composer. The music has the rare qualities of imagination and atmosphere, and is of genuine poetic feeling. Around ideas suggested by Housman's poems of the same title the composer has woven some graceful ideas, working them out in musicianly style and with some very individual orchestral effects. The impression left by the music is that of an undeveloped individuality, which might have developed strikingly in future works. – *Evening News.*

Of the many settings of A.E. Housman's 'A Shropshire Lad,' one of the most successful, though not yet the most popular, was that of the late Lieut. George Butterworth in the form of two song cycles. To these he wrote a kind of orchestral epilogue, which was produced at the Queen's Hall Promenade Concert last night by Sir Henry Wood. Described as a rhapsody, which it is in form, the work is elegiac in character, reminiscent and full of longing. Apart from its thematic connection with the song cycles it has little in common with them, and might well be a tribute to a departed friend or a recollection of departed days. Its delicacy of outline and texture makes it a difficult work to appreciate to the full at a first hearing, though it has a sensuous charm which could not but be felt by the most casual listener. Perhaps not so strikingly original as the works on which it is based, it is, nevertheless, a work quite out of the ordinary in inspiration and execution, and intensifies the regret that a composer of such rare talent and beauty of thought should have been taken away so early in his career. – *Evening Standard.*

None of the unfamiliar British music presented attracted more sympathetic attention than the Orchestral Rhapsody, 'A Shropshire Lad,' composed by the late Lieut. Geo. Butterworth, M.C., whose untimely death in France is one of the innumerable tragedies of the war.... At Leeds the work made a favourable impression, and greatly helped to establish the reputation of the composer as a coming man. The impression of refined feeling then made was deepened upon the present occasion. – *Musical Times.*

.... In the course of a close study of folksongs, Lieut. Butterworth had acquired an idiom that, without being founded on them, reproduced something of their character and had therefore a thoroughly English flavour. The Rhapsody is a good example of this, a meditative pastoral with peculiar sadness that is so fascinating in the poems. – *Pall Mall Gazette.*

George Butterworth had more than technique, as proved by many beautiful ideas enshrined in the composition under notice. His musical description of a spring day is delightful in its ethereal suggestion. After the work had been played and while the tragedy of the young composer was fresh in the memory, instinctively came to mind Milton's words:- *'Such notes as, warbled to the string, Drew iron tears down Pluto's cheek.'* - *The Queen.*

The first performance in London on Thursday of the late Lieut. Butterworth's Rhapsody, 'A Shropshire Lad,' made one realise two things – how difficult it is to get a new orchestral work produced in London and what a poetical composer we have lost by the war, for Lieut. Butterworth was killed fighting for his country last August twelvemonth. .... The composer is best known by

his settings of A.E. Housman's poems 'The Shropshire Lad.'.
.. The music is singularly intimate in expression, and seems to pulsate with treasured memories and tender emotion viewed thro' a veil of sadness. The piece might be taken as in memory of the composer's snapped career. – *The Referee.*

Produced as long ago as the last Leeds Festival before the war, we ought to have heard Lieut. George Butterworth's Rhapsody on songs from Housman's 'Shropshire Lad' months and years before this in London. Daintiness, bloom and beauty – the beauty of a warm spring day – are the features of this imaginative and modest little composition. Scholarship, of course, and the resourcefulness that keeps clear of conventionality, went to its making, but it is essentially light as a Rhapsody of Spring should be. There is atmosphere in it – British atmosphere; melody in it – British melody. And there is any amount of promise, which alas! can never be fulfilled. – *The Sunday Times.*

Since these concerts the Rhapsody has been played at the Queen's Hall (Sir Henry Wood), at the Albert Hall (Mr. Landon Ronald) and at the Queen's Hall (Mr. Adrian Boult). Also at Bristol, Bradford, Manchester, Liverpool and Leeds. The programme of Mr. Adrian Boult's Concert contained the following note. – A.K.B. March, 1918.

"English music has suffered an irreparable loss by the death of George Butterworth just at the moment when – as the *Shropshire Lad* Rhapsody shows – he had mastered the technique of his individual style. No composer ever saturated himself more completely in the study of folk-song. He was the most assiduous of collectors, and was also an accomplished dancer of traditional dances. He wrote little, and was a severe critic of his own work. The Rhapsody, which is 'in the nature of an orchestral epilogue' to the composer's two sets of the songs from the poem by A.E. Housman, is a notable contribution to modern English music not only for its poetry and beauty, but for its method of construction. Its form is original, and arises naturally out of its emotion; that is, out of its musical and psychological character, not out of a literary programme. It needs no literary explanation, and is admirably lucid and perfectly balanced. It opens with an introduction based on a single phrase; the main section presents two contrasting themes, one of quiet character given out by the hautboys, the other, assigned first to the trumpet, a broken arpeggio in slow triplets. These are worked together to a passionate climax, after which the music subsides and the work ends with a return to the theme of the introduction.

Slight as it may appear, judged by mere duration, this Rhapsody should be a landmark in the history of our music, for it is the first work of symphonic type in which the new and characteristic idiom evolved out of the study of folk-song has been treated in a new musical form proper in itself, and this too with a polished perfection of style that has eliminated every superfluous note. It is deeply passionate, yet never rhetorical or exaggerated, perfect in balance both of structure and of orchestral colour, always consistent and homogenous in style, without ever either lapsing into a traditional commonplace or disfiguring an emotional point by the least awkward or uncertain stroke. Other composers have struggled, some are still struggling, towards the solution of the new technique. Here, for a few brief moments, we see its accomplishment."

NOTICES OF WORKS

Reprinted from The Music Student, December, 1913.
Modern British Song Writers by Rutland Boughton.

George Butterworth. A new song-composer of the first order! That is my feeling after a fortnight's careful and constant study of George Butterworth's two books of songs from 'A Shropshire Lad.'

The rustic, ironic, and beautiful verses of A.E. Housman have attracted several makers of songs, even, alas! those song-makers who furbish up an apparently new song whenever a publisher can be found to give it a chance; but no song-maker has so exactly fitted these verses with their inevitable music as George Butterworth. Indeed, no one need try in future; Housman's art has been mated to its perfect musical counterpart: in Butterworth's music there are the same amazing restraint, and the same simple lyrism and the same terrible beauty which one finds in the verses.

Consider the question of restraint. Are not most songs, especially most modern songs, full of notes? Does it not appear as if the composer's object is to cover as 'effective' a vocal range as possible, with special top or bottom notes to draw away attention from the thought (or lack of thought) in the verse, and concentrate upon the lust for vocal fatness of tone which is the curse of ten singers out of twelve? Again are not the greater number of song accompaniments fairly choked with notes? Now one of Butterworth's ideas in these songs seems to have been to get rid of as many notes as possible. They are like the songs of Franz in their exquisite refinement. They are, as an artist suggested to me the other day, like the most beautiful

Japanese print in that they contain no single melodic line or harmonic note which is not necessary and inevitable.

Look at the first song in the first book...Why, the words themselves are a Japanese picture! The music of this extract occupies sixteen bars. The vocal part is entirely melodious, free, fragrant, and original in outline; it occupies the space of a minor tenth, being unusually spreading for Butterworth. But the extraordinary compression of thought in the accompaniment is worth the study of any song-writer, ancient or modern. During these sixteen bars there are but seven chords, the interest of the accompaniment being almost entirely concentrated in the curving, swaying, be-blossomed thematic line, which calls up in one's feelings all that the flowering cherry-tree calls up in one's thoughts.

Consider next the simplicity of these songs. The composer has clearly made the most careful study of English folk-song. I do not mean to say that he has consciously adopted folk-phrases, although one of these songs is avowedly a traditional tune; I mean rather that he has been so steeped in the spirit of English folk-song that he naturally and spontaneously expresses himself in similar terms. I would give my ears to be able to do the like. For in these days of transition from the evils of industrialism and professionalism to the joys of a freed people, it is a glad sign that the natural musical line of folk-melody should be used again. We who have our minds cumbered with the upholstery of an elaborate technic will be of no use to ourselves or anyone else in the days which must soon be if England is ever again to be a place worth living in. Butterworth's songs are entirely free of such elaboration. His songs stand in relation to the songs of his contemporaries much as a naked Adonis stands in relation to the modern English inhuman being, encased in starch, leather, and other signs of serfdom. A wonderful example of Butterworth's simplicity is the song 'Is my team still a-ploughing?' Four verses with four different aspects of the same thought have each the same music and the same accompaniment of the most primitive kind; but it is entirely convincing, and makes one wonder that so many of us should go so far afield for effect when such beautiful things may be done in such simple ways.

The third chief feature of the songs is their terrible beauty. This, of course, was inevitable, if the composer were to be in the least true to his poet. Tragedy underlies all the greatest art which does not attain to, or is not content in, a mystic mood; and tragedy is the very marrow of 'The Shropshire Lad.' Some artists are able to find a glory when once they passed beyond the Valley of the Shadow of Materialism. 'The Shropshire Lad' never leaves the Valley, even in such apparently happy moments as the 'Song of the Cherry-Tree.' Tragedy, therefore, is the keynote of Butterworth's art, as we have it here – not the monstrous terrors of Aeschylus – but the resigned beauty that goes with hopelessness. A far nobler frame of mind than the smug, greasy content, which exudes from the face of the materialist, whose bank-balance assures him that all is well with his own mean world!

How wonderfully the iron of gloom may be transmuted to the irony of beauty may be discovered in these songs of Butterworth's. I have not even alluded to those I most enjoy; they are all so fine that choice is a matter of personal taste. But of one thing I am certain; the volume published in 1912 shows that the composer had grown since the previous year when he issued the first set of songs, and for the future any publication of new songs by George Butterworth will be an event in the musical world.

Reprinted from The Musical Standard, 29ᵗʰ July, 1916.
Some Notable British Music by W. Wells-Harrison.
George Butterworth, Songs From "A Shropshire Lad."
(Two Cycles).

A. E. Housman's book of verses, 'A Shropshire Lad,' has appealed to many modern song writers, and not a few have scored successes in the setting of them. Their influence is not by any means difficult to account for, as it is fair to say that no poet has succeeded in touching the entire gamut of simple countryside emotion, in laying bare their hopes, joys, fears, sorrows and passions in so few and simple words. Dr. Arthur Somervell has written a scholarly and extremely effective song-cycle to a selection of Housman's words and some settings by Graham Peel are musicianly and original both in thought and utterance.

It often happens in music that many composers set the same poem, but we are not infrequently inclined to think of one setting as the inevitable musical clothing for the poet's thought. The 'Erl King' of Schubert absolutely puts a really fine song of Loewe in the shade, whilst few would be inclined to replace Schumann's 'Two Grenadiers' by Wagner's intensely dramatic version of the same poem. So in the case of these verses of Housman's, whilst we can enjoy the musical beauty and wealth of invention displayed by Somervell, Peel and others in their settings, I, for one, am bound to admit that an unknown composer, George Butterworth by name, has given us the inevitable musical counterpart to the verses. It is always comforting to find oneself in agreement with contemporary thought, and after forming my opinion upon these songs some time ago I was pleased to find a glowing tribute to their effectiveness in the pages of *The Music Student* from no less an authority than Mr. Rutland Boughton.

If asked who Mr. Butterworth is and what other work he has written, I am bound to confess that my information is of the scantiest possible description. So far as my knowledge goes, he is a Yorkshireman and a son of the one-time general manager of the North Eastern Railway Company, whilst as for his other work, I know but one, namely, an orchestral rhapsody, founded upon a theme from one of these songs, entitled 'A Shropshire Lad,' which was played at the Leeds Festival of 1913. As a usual occurrence at these gatherings, the work was badly placed on the programme, coming, as it did, immediately after the lunch interval, when one's faculties are busily engaged upon the all-absorbing problem of how best to digest a hasty meal, and it had the further disadvantage of having to follow a magnificent performance of Verdi's 'Requiem,' one of the outstanding features of the festival. Personally, I was able to enjoy the work despite the efforts of a couple of tough sandwiches and a bottle of bad Bass. It is one which should appeal to Mr. Julian Clifford and Mr. Dan Godfrey, who might well give it a performance. These two conductors have enormous opportunities of doing good to British music, and, to their eternal credit, they never neglect them.

Coming to the songs themselves, one is first of all struck with what is, perhaps, their chief characteristic, namely, economy of means. There is very little that is decorative in them, and they are for the most part simply made a means of conveying the diction of the lines. A friend of mine on being shown them summed up what I am afraid the general impression of them would be in the pregnant words: 'Why, they are most of them not songs at all!' Quite true; they are not in the ordinary sense of songs as we generally understand them, namely, verses set to more or less appropriate music, but, in point of fact, simply a musical intensification of Housman's words. And as the poet expresses himself in tense and economical lines, so the composer clothes them with music which is their exact counterpart in this respect.

There is no necessity to discuss the songs in detail, but it is better to endeavour to discover the salient points of each. They are published in two cycles by Augener and Co., at a price which brings them well within reach of all who require to make a thorough study.

'Bredon Hill' is an example of what can be achieved with the use of a tiny germinal phrase, but the whole song is necessarily the most elaborate of the eleven because of its poetic texture. The next song, 'O Fair Enough are Sky and Plain,' is extremely simple and perfectly free as regards rhythm, but has a poetic little thought running through the second stanza. 'When the Lad for Longing Sighs' is folk-song-like in character and its melody is lyrical and beautiful, whilst 'On the Idle Hill of Summer' shows Butterworth at his best. It is true that the song is a little fuller with regard to material, but it is equally true that such a course is rendered imperative by the poem. The final song of this cycle is again of folk character.

The first number of the next set, 'Loveliest of Trees,' has a texture entirely woven out of the initial motive, whilst the following one again returns to the extreme simplicity of utterance. 'Think No More Lad,' also makes a virtue of this same treatment, until at the final stanza the composer involves an accompanimental figure out of the meagre chords employed in the opening, whilst another of folk character is 'The Lads in their Hundreds.'

The final song is without doubt the gem of the whole collection. In the poem, 'Is My Team Ploughing?' Housman achieved a drama of intensely moving quality in three brief verses. This the composer has treated in a masterly fashion, perfectly free in declamation and never hindered by the accompaniment, which is meagre beyond description. It is none the less one of the most moving things in the whole range of song literature.

Let me state, by way of conclusion, that I have no desire to compare these songs with other settings of the same poems. Comparisons are odious at all times, but these songs stand beyond the pale of comparison because they are things apart. The songs of Somervell and Peel are fine music, in this respect, perhaps, a good deal better than these, but here Butterworth uses the poetry in his own particular way, and the tense and at times almost crude expression brings out all the passion and pathos of the simple rustic mind.

Drawing-room singers beware! Do not touch them, they are far too outspoken, too elemental for the taste of your audiences. Their appeal is far beyond those who are hide-bound by the false polish of modern society. They bring us face to face with Nature, and they need a singer with a soul.

Note: The original hardback volume ran to127 pages, its dimensions being 10" x 7 ¼". Whenever possible, I have kept to the original as regards features of punctuation, underlining and layout. Significant abbreviations used:

AKB – Alexander Kaye Butterworth;

D – Dorothea Ionides;

MEB – May Butterworth;

ROM - R.O. Morris;

HPA – Hugh Allen;

RVW – Ralph Vaughan Williams;

RL – Reginald Lennard;

LEB – Lucy Broadwood;

CJS – Cecil Sharpe;

HJW – Henry Wood.

Wayne Smith, 31ˢᵗ January 2015.

DELITTLE, FENWICK & CO.,
FINE ART PRINTERS
YORK AND LONDON

Printed in Great Britain
by Amazon